Revisiting Mahesh Dattani

Edited by
Vijay Kumar Sharma
Shyam Samtani

ATLANTIC
PUBLISHERS & DISTRIBUTORS (P) LTD

Published by
ATLANTIC

PUBLISHERS & DISTRIBUTORS (P) LTD

7/22, Ansari Road, Darya Ganj, New Delhi-110002
Phones : +91-11-40775252, 23273880, 23275880, 23280451
Fax : +91-11-23285873
Web : www.atlanticbooks.com
E-mail : orders@atlanticbooks.com

Branch Office
5, Nallathambi Street, Wallajah Road, Chennai-600002
Phones : +91-44-64611085, 32413319
E-mail : chennai@atlanticbooks.com

Reprint 2018

Printed in India at Nice Printing Press, A-33/3A, Site-IV,
Industrial Area, Sahibabad, Ghaziabad, U.P.

Foreword

I have often said, on several occasions, that Mahesh and I are like an old married couple in the theatrical space.

We have worked together for over 20 years, have produced 5 plays, vastly varied in theme and form, have made and modified, experimented with and exhumed, altercated about and altered, censored and celebrated, every one of them, from inception to maturity, have learnt how to push and challenge each other, and finally how to extract the best from each other.

By freeing our imaginations and walking on roads less travelled, but especially by putting our egos to one side, we have travelled together.

Of course, the writer and director have to be on the same page (the director has to resonate with the theme and content of the writer's material) but this process of working on a piece of writing together, to create the final product, is a literary process peculiar only to theatre and cinema. It is a co-creation like no other, because it is only in the playing out of the material on stage that the playwright really knows whether his work *works*!

It may all sound brilliant on paper, but unless the dialogues come 'trippingly on the tongue' they may as well stay on the page. So too the characters. They may sound fascinating to read, but must sparkle with equal richness and complexity when played. The acid test for the playwright is when the play hits the boards!

Some of the most exciting plays have been born out of such collaborations, one of the greatest being that between Elia Kazan and Arthur Miller, who shared the same artistic vision, while holding radically divergent political views. Kazan directed and shaped those legendary plays to become the classics that they are today, whittling and polishing the script till it was at its leanest, potent best.

My theatre company was set up primarily to promote and platform Indian writing in English, to create a body of work that was contemporary and original, so that we could tell our own stories, which were uniquely Indian in spirit, yet moored in a universal context. And also, to then take these productions abroad, and open them up to a global audience to gauge how well they fared on the world stage.

Mahesh's plays are strongly Indian in flavour and tone, but whatever their themes, they always hook an audience because of their strong emotional appeal.

We have performed his plays all over India and across the globe and they have struck a chord with people everywhere, be they about over-the-hill Bharatnatyam dancers (*Dance Like a Man* with 520 shows and still dancing!) or sexual abuse (*30 Days in September* that has broken barriers and performed in several repressed socio-cultures across the world) or about ageing Divas—from the world of theatre and the trauma of the subcontinental partition (*Where Did I Leave My Purdah?*)—to India's first original play on homosexuality (*On a Muggy Night in Mumbai*). All these productions broke new ground in one way or another.

I think we are both attracted to subjects that delve into socio-cultural issues but that still manage to engage and entertain, (because this is an art form which is not complete unless it is a shared experience with an audience) and the challenge is how to marry these two goals. Over the years this challenge remains, especially in the light of competing with a burgeoning type of theatre that aims largely to entertain and please.

In closing, I need to mention two of his most powerful plays—*Tara* and *Bravely Fought the Queen*—which I feel still haven't received their due.

I hope one day to explore and perform both these, but as of now, Mahesh and I are both lost in the rarefied world of Indian classical music and an era gone by, in search of India's first great musical rockstar and her triumphs and travails…the fiery and fabulous Gauhar Jaan, undisputed queen of the Thumri!

Lillete Dubey
Mumbai, India

Introduction

T.S. Eliot observes that for as great a writer as Shakespeare it is likely that we may not be right; therefore, let us change our stand of being wrong every time. In other words, there is always some scope for multi-dimensional, myriad-minded interpretation of his works which defies possibilities of concretization of opinions. As a matter of fact, creation and so also the interpretation of a work of art depends on an individual's intuitive perception, his sensibility and susceptibility, the horizons of his education and orientation, the experiences and traumas of life. One just needs to appreciate the perspective of the author which is conditioned and chiselled by the circumstances he is placed in.

India is a vast country with multi-lingual, cultural, religious and regional diversity manifesting itself in literature supposed to be the mirror of the society. Be it a poet, a novelist or a playwright, the medium reflects the patriarchal socio-familial set-up, gender construct, marginalization of women struggling for space, the silenced voice of the subaltern, communal conflicts, rapes and violence, child sex-abuse, drug peddling, fusion of chromosomes resulting into LGBT (lesbian, gay, bisexual, transgender), identity crises, etc. leading to problems like split personality, neurosis, paranoia, mania, phobia and such other obsessive or compulsive disorders. A creative writer, whatever society he lives in, cannot keep his lids down or ears plugged to the surroundings. His instincts impel him to use his medium to express and ventilate his feelings, ire or responses. The purpose may be to serve a clarion call to the dormant consciousness or jolt the complacent social apathy.

Mahesh Dattani, one of the most prolific of the contemporary playwrights, has looked around with woken eyes and presented a large variety of social phenomena one is confronted with in everyday walk of life. One needs the courage of conviction, ability to array thoughts in communicative idiom, vision to create living characters, vibrant dynamics of theatre, including the stagecraft, multi-levelled stage, acoustics, light dimmer/reflectors and props. Let alone the theatrical skills, Mahesh Dattani is a trained classical dancer; he has an ear for music too. His plays have created both ripples and rapids in the world of theatre, not only in India but also abroad. With his second play, *Dance Like a Man*, Dattani shot into what can possibly be termed as blazing fame. Erin Mee, the celebrated theatre director, who is associated with the Department of Theatre in New York University, included Dattani's play, *Tara,* in her syllabus for a class on Indian Performance. Mahesh Dattani, winner of the pestigious Sahitya Akademi Award has never looked back. In fact, he has carved for himself a place in the history of Indian English Drama.

Dattani has been fairly audacious in staging themes which are considered taboo in the social structure. One can deal with such themes in a novel, which is supposed to have a wide canvass and can be read in an easy armchair inside a secluded room; but to present such issues, which implicate the law of the land, on the stage needs the iron nerves and sinews of a Dattani. There is neither any obscenity nor vulgarity in expression characteristic of a red light area while dealing with sex-related issues. Dattani's treatment is subtle and dialogues of his characters catchy.

In some of his plays such as *Where Did I Leave My Purdah?*, Dattani advocates the cause of the theatre, in which the protagonist prefers the theatre to films: "Your cinema is too small for me.... Only theatre deserves me." His latest play, *The Big Fat City*, boxes multiple themes which beget one another like the medieval cycles of stories. The audience, so also the reader, marvels at such ingenuity of the author. We are indeed grateful to Mahesh Dattani for providing us the manuscripts of his then unpublished plays, *Where Did I Leave My Purdah?* and *The Big Fat City*. This enabled us to get papers from scholars on these plays. He has been helpful in other matters too.

We express our gratitude to Ms. Lillete Dubey for embellishing this volume by writing the Foreword. We thank the contributors for their papers without which the book could not have seen the light of the day. We owe thanks to Atlantic Publishers also for printing this volume. We sincerely hope that it would help the students in their academic pursuits.

Vijay Kumar Sharma
Shyam Samtani

Contents

Contributors

Abhinaba Chatterjee received a diploma in Translation Studies from IGNOU, New Delhi, in 2013. Chatterjee has published in *The Criterion* and *Lapis Lazuli*. His interest is Teaching Methodology. Presently he is employed in the Ministry of Finance, Government of India.

Priti Bhatt has been teaching Literature and Language for more than two decades. She has published in many journals and books. Currently, she teaches English at Government Nirbhaya Singh Patel Science College, Indore.

Shyam Samtani taught English Literature for more than four decades. A Visiting Professor in School of Languages, Devi Ahilya University, Indore for more than two decades, Samtani had been a Resource Person at the Refresher Courses in Indore, Jabalpur, and Rewa. He presented papers and Chaired various sessions in national and international seminars. He has published more than 35 papers in research journals and books. Having published and travelled widely, Samtani retired as the Head and Professor, PG Department of English and Research Centre, Indore Christian College, Indore.

Pranav Joshipura has been teaching English Literature for more than two decades. He has great interest in drama. He has an M.Phil. on works of Girish Karnad and a Ph.D. on Mahesh Dattani's plays. He has two published books and many papers. He has been a resource person at many refresher courses, seminars and workshops. Currently, he is pursuing UGC Major Research Project on Diasporic Indian theatre and is an Associate Professor at Uma Arts and Nathiba Commerce Mahila College, Gandhinagar, Gujarat.

Tausheeh Abbasi has a Ph.D. on the works of Mahesh Dattani. Other areas of her interest are Linguistics and Phonetics.

Currently, she is an Assistant Professor of English, Government Holkar Science College, Indore.

Nisha Tiwari has an M.Phil. from Jamia Millia Islamia. She studied at the University of Hawaii at Minoa under the Fulbright Foreign Language Teaching Assistant Program. Her research and teaching interests include third world feminism and postcolonial studies. She has been working in the Dept. of English at Bharati College, University of Delhi. She teaches courses on English Restoration, Modernism, Indian Literature in English and Feminism.

Deepa Diddi has a Ph.D. in Indo-Canadian Literature. She has presented a number of papers at national and international forums. A spiritual healer and an exponent in Yoga, Diddi has conducted workshops and seminars on meditation, stress and anger management for various corporates. She has been a leading graphologist for eminent business houses. She has been teaching for the last 22 years in various colleges across the country in Pune, Jalandhar, Gurgaon, Faridabad and New Delhi.

Deepa Vanjani has been a freelance columnist for the *Hindustan Times* and the *Times of India* and has been writing for *Confluence*, a magazine published from London. She has presented papers in national and international seminars. Vanjani has been a visiting faculty at Educational Media Research Centre for M.Sc. Electronics and at School of Languages, Devi Ahilya University, Indore for M.Phil. Currently, she is the Head of English Dept. at PMB Gujarati Science College, Indore.

Gunasekharan Dharmaraja is the official translator of Mahesh Dattani from English to Tamil and has more than 60 presentations and publications. He has delivered lectures in India, Bhutan, Nepal, USA, Thailand and South Africa. He is an active life member of Nepal English Language Teachers' Association and is a notable political writer. He is also strategic facilitator for the Ministry of Basic Education, South Africa. He has been in teaching since 2003 and is, currently, a post-doctoral fellow at the University of KwaZulu-Natal, South Africa.

Jasmine Dordi is a gold medalist from Devi Ahilya University, Indore. An ardent educationalist, Dordi has taught in different institutions, including S.B. Arts and Commerce College in Aurangabad. She has keen interest in Irish Drama and directed a production of *Arms and the Man* also.

Vimmie Manoj is an academician, artist and poet. She has taught English for 8 years at degree and P.G. levels. Apart from that, she has made presentations in many national and international conferences. Her papers have been published in books and journals. She specializes in Gender and Post-Colonial studies. She has published many poems too. As a global artist, her paintings have been showcased in many national and international galleries.

Bandana Burman writes poems, short stories and literary criticism. Currently, she teaches English at Prestige Institute of Management and Research, Indore.

Nutan Kulshreshtha is a Gold Medalist from Dayal Bagh Educational Institute, Agra. Having published more than two dozen papers in prestigious research journals, and participated in various conferences, Kulshreshtha has translated poetry from Hindi into English, which was published in *Indian Literature*. Currently, she teaches English at Govt. P.G. College, Guna.

Usha Jain has made presentations in many national and International seminars, including one in Manchester. Also, she has published widely. She specializes in Indian Writing in English and American Literature. She has been teaching English for the last more than thirty years. Currently, she teaches English at Shri Atal Bihari Vajpayee Government Arts and Commerce College, Indore.

Manik Sambre has published widely and has been the Chair, Board of Studies (English). She has also been the Dean, Faculty of Arts, Devi Ahilya University, Indore. She has a Post Graduate Diploma in Teaching of English from CIEFL, Hyderabad. She has been a resource person at many seminars and conferences. Currently, she teaches English at Shri Atal Bihari Vajpayee Government Arts and Commerce College, Indore. Her academic interests include Modern Critical Theory.

Jyoti Taneja has participated in national and international seminars. She has been a member of the Jury for Online Creative Poetry Competition organized by the Braham Kumaris' Organization, Mount Abu. Apart from being in the Dept. of Higher Education, M.P. since 1994, she has been teaching English at Shri Atal Bihari Vajpayee Government Arts and Commerce College, Indore.

Urbashi Barat has authored three books, edited two more and published more than 70 research articles. She was formerly the Professor and Head, Department of Postgraduate Studies and Research Centre in English, the Director, UGC Centre for Ambedkar Studies and Director, UGC Centre for Gandhian Studies, Rani Durgavati University, Jabalpur. Areas of her research interests include Twentieth Century Literature in English, Women's Studies, especially women's drama and ELT.

Shachi Sood is a Ph.D. on Mahesh Dattani and has published six papers so far. She has been teaching English at Baba Ghulam Shah Badshah University, Rajouri (J & K). Her academic interests include gender studies.

Rashmi Sahi is a freelance writer. She writes fiction and on academic issues. She has been on the advisory and review Board of *Oracle*, an international journal of English Language and Literature and *The Literary Icon*. She is the consultant editor of Siyahi, a literary organization. She is also a visiting faculty at Hong Kong University School of Professional and Continuing Education. Currently, she is the Head, English Department, St. Stephen's College Prep School, Hong Kong.

Lalit Ratoniya is a Research Scholar in English at Rani Durgavati University, Jabalpur. Currently, he is engaged in Ph.D. on Mahesh Dattani's plays.

1

The Subjugated Speaks: The Plays of Mahesh Dattani

Abhinaba Chatterjee

Mahesh Dattani is among the few Indian writers writing in English to perceive the continued violence of postcolonial discourses and propose an all-inclusive democracy-to-come by giving voice to the subjugated. The subjugated can be equalized with the subalterns in the sense that they are socially ostracized and suppressed.

Subjugation creates anomie in society because it hampers the natural growth of human beings by repressing their inborn instincts and imposing restrictions which, in turn, may lead to a state of neurosis and ultimate mental breakdown resulting in psychopathic problems for the community. Therefore, the subjugated becomes subject of psychological studies for writers who probe deep into the psyche of such characters. While some characters are depicted as vocal against the repression, others shrink into silence which is "the ancient language of defeat".

Dattani's representation of subjugation is depicted through the conflict of the traditional cultural thought and modern western discourses. For Dattani, social suppositions are always different from the realities of life. For example, one cannot expect a son always to be obedient or a blind follower of his parents. This conflict is brought out brilliantly in the play *Where There's a Will* (1988).

In the play, Dattani takes up the issues of the patriarchal code. Indian society has been a very traditional society with strong patriarchal value. Fathers have desired sons because they are supposed to carry forward the name of the family, and because in their sons, fathers have hoped to live out their dreams and aspirations; thereby demanding unquestioning obedience from the son and subsequently denying the opportunity for independent growth to the son.

This issue is taken up through the character of a supposedly "self-made" successful industrialist, Hasmukh Mehta. This patriarch is the supreme malcontent, who tries to dictate his son Ajit, because he would not toe his father's line. When they talk to one another, Hasmukh is blunt and contemptuous, and Ajit is defiant. In a series of revealing conversations, the dramatist makes their attitudes clear:

> Ajit: Don't I have any rights at all?
>
> Hasmukh: You have the right to listen to my advice and obey my orders.
>
> Ajit: Thank you. You are so generous. I could kiss your feet.
>
> Hasmukh: There's no need to do that, just polish my shoes every morning and I will be happy.
>
> Ajit: You will never be happy. Not until all of us dance to your tune. And I will never do that.
>
> Hasmukh: Don't be so stubborn.
>
> Ajit: You are stubborn too.
>
> Hasmukh: I'm stubborn because I know I'm right. You're stubborn because you are a nincompoop.

Hasmukh feels that his son needs 'seasoning' to make him fit to run the company when he would no longer be there. The conversation reveals the dominating tendency of Hasmukh.

> Hasmukh: …I will retire one day, either from the company or from this world. What will become of you then? I have to season you now. You need seasoning.
>
> Ajit: Seasoning! What do you mean seasoning? I'm not a block of wood.

Hasmukh: You are raw! Under all that pressure in the office, you will bend. You will break. That's why I'm toughening you up. Somebody tough has to be around to run the show.

Ajit: Your show, you mean.

Hasmukh: Well, later it will be your show.

Ajit: No, it won't. That's what you're making sure of.

Hasmukh: What do you mean?

Ajit: I mean that you want to run the show, play Big Boss as long as you can. Or as long as God permits. And when all of a sudden, you are "called to a better world", you will still want to play Big Boss. And you can do it through me. In short, you want me to be you.

Hasmukh: I should have prayed for a daughter. Yes, I want you to be me! What's wrong with being me?

Ajit: And what becomes of me? The real me. I mean if I am you, then where am I?

Hasmukh: Nowhere! That is just my point! If you are you, then you are *nowhere*. You are *nothing*. Just a big zero. No matter what you do, you'll remain a zero. Over the years you'll just keep adding zeroes to your zero. Zero, zero, zero. On their own, the zeroes don't mean a thing. But if there's a number one standing before all those zeroes, then they really add up to a lot.

Ajit: And I suppose you think you're the number one in front of my zeroes.

Hasmukh: Yes! Now you understand! You do understand? At last!

This conversation has dual implications. On the one hand, it reflects the strong desire of the older generation to preserve its authority over the young and the determined bid of the young to break free of this patriarchal code. On the other hand, this conversation also depicts the traditional 'civilizing mission' of the imperial power over the subalterns. Looked at the play from this point of view, the character of Ajit is that of the empire writing back.

A similar tone of the desire of the older generation to dominate the young is heard in *Final Solutions*:

> Aruna (to Javed): Please try to understand. We have nothing against you. It is only that, we have our ways and customs and—and—we are all equal. There is no doubt. We respect your religion and wish you well. Why, we have friends who are.... Smita has so many friends who are not.... All religion is one. Only the ways to God are many.
>
> (Ramnik cannot control his laughter. He laughs out aloud.)
>
> Aruna: I was not being funny.
>
> Ramnik: (laughing) All religion is one. The ways to God are many. I used to say that to you.
>
> Aruna: I can also laugh at you.
>
> Ramnik: You don't have to. I do it for you.
>
> Smita: Mummy, I want to fill up water and go back to sleep.
>
> Aruna (to Javed): We don't allow anyone to fill our drinking water. No outsiders.
>
> Smita: Mummy, please!
>
> Aruna: We bathe our god with it, Smita. It has to be pure. It must not be contaminated.
>
> Smita: You are making it worse by explaining.
>
> Aruna: But that is the real reason. (To Javed) So there is no need to feel offended.
>
> Ramnik: No?
>
> Aruna (to Ramnik): Not at all. How we feel in our house is our business. If they cannot respect it, they must learn to tolerate it.
>
> Bobby: Yes, of course. We understand.
>
> Ramnik (to Aruna): When I can't tolerate it, how can they?
>
> (Ramnik exits)

Smita: Mummy, thank you for making me feel like a rat in a hole.

[Pause]

Aruna: What makes you think you have all the answers? Don't you have any respect for who you are? I shudder to think what will become of your children. What kind of sanskar will you give them when you don't have any yourself? It's all very well to have progressive ideas. But are you progressing or are you drifting? God knows, I don't want all this violence. How can I when I won't harm a goat or a chicken? But to throw everything just like that? Doesn't it mean anything to you? For so many generations we have preserved our sanskar because we believe it is the truth. It is the way shown to us by our saints. We must know no other path. And I will not have it all perish to accommodate someone else's faith. I have enough faith and pride to see that it doesn't happen. I shall uphold what I believe is the truth.

Smita: It is the truth only because you believe in it.

Aruna: No! I will not accept that. Not from you.

Smita: Why not?

Aruna: I will not!

Smita: You have to face it. You have to admit that you are wrong!

Aruna: You cannot tell me I am wrong!

Smita: Why not?

Aruna: Because—because I will not accept that from someone who is not proud of her inheritance.

(Smita sits down, placing the brass pot limply on her lap.)

Aruna: You cannot criticize what you are running away from. You will be prejudiced.

Smita: How can you expect me to be proud of something which stifles everything else? It stifles me. Yes! May be I am prejudiced because I do not belong. But not belonging makes things so clear. I can see so clearly how wrong you are. You accuse me of running away from my religion? May be I am—embarrassed, Mummy. Yes. Maybe I shouldn't be. What if I did what you do? Praying and fasting and—purifying myself all day. Would you have listened to me if I told you were wrong? You will say yes, because you are certain I wouldn't say that then. All right, so we both are prejudiced, so what do you want to do? Shall we all go back to sleep?

Aruna: You said it stifles you?

Smita: What?

Aruna: Does being a Hindu stifle you?

Smita: No, living with one does.

Besides the recurring theme of the conflict between the generations, in *Final Solutions*, Dattani interprets Indianness as a religious nationalism counterpoised to colonial modernity. Retorting to her daughter's request to accommodate her Muslim friends, Aruna's long speech above on the legitimacy of her convictions is Dattani's analysis of the emphasis on tradition that marks the discourse of the religious right in India from pre-independence days to the present.

Partha Chatterjee's famous thesis in response to Benedict Anderson's theory of nationalism draws our attention to the psychological aspect of the situation. Chatterjee says that the indigenous imagination divides the world into two spheres: the material and the spiritual. The more one adapts to the former, the more they protect the latter. The sovereignty makes the inner space of culture and religion a base from which to launch a rigorous nationalist project. Failure to conform to the norms of *Sanskar* is like drifting away from the imagined community and its ideals. This normativity severely limits friendship/hospitality, as it imposes on these individuals' different masks and roles.

In *The Presentation of Self in Everyday Life*, Erving Goffman compares individuals interacting in society to actors playing their roles on stage: just as actors act out a readymade script, a social individual has to follow certain codes of communication to successfully manage his/her interactions. Moreover, an actor cannot act out their role independently, and has to change their posture accordingly with significant changes in the co-actor's pose. Social identities are all about one's roles and poses and the masks one uses. These are not static references but variable, a function of the nuanced changes in the behaviour of the other, and this is effortlessly presented in Dattani's play through the use of a chorus putting masks on and off.

Seven Steps Around the Fire is a tale of violated hospitality and denied justice. Politically unqualified *hijras* like Anarkali, Kamla and Champa live a nude life in the postcolonial nation, where the Ramayana myth about their origin is dismissed by the contemptuous remarks of the Superintendent of Police that they are "all just castrated degenerate men". Dattani reminds here that the *sanskar,* the postcolonial nation exalts is a reworking of existing culture, where the aberrant elements are to be excluded/ denied to create a glorious and stable self-image of the imagined community. Within the postcolonial nationalist discourse of Indianness, the figure of the queer is disgraced and interpreted as western aberration to ensure moral self-assurance of the nation.

Uma Rao, a researcher (the daughter-in-law of the Deputy Commissioner and the wife of the SP) goes to the male section of the Central Jail in Bangalore to interview Anarkali, a *hijra* arrested on a charge of murdering Kamala, another member of her community. Dattani very cleverly weaves the net of suspense to keep the audience on the edges of their seats. The play is not only about the murder investigation of a *hijra*, but about their social positioning and the social setup where a *hijra* cannot crave her feelings and emotions beyond the patterns and boundaries recommended by the society. These individuals face threat or violence because of their position in the society. The play depicts the social space of hostility faced by them and the vindictive social responses that they experience.

Various characters are shown interacting with *hijras*. They have their pre-established notions of hatred regarding the *hijras* and do not want to change those ideas. Their interaction with the general society and other individuals does not lead to any kind of happiness. Anarkali scratches the face of Kamla with a knife, because she knows that they can only be subject to hatred in the society and if someone loves a *hijra* that can just lead to some tragedy. This is what ultimately happens:

> ...So many times I warned her. First I thought Salim was taking her for his own pleasure. When she told me about Subbu, madam, I tried to stop her. I fought with her. I scratched her face, hoping she will become ugly and Subbu will forget her. He wanted to marry her....I was there at their wedding....she gave me that picture to show to Champa. I saw the men coming for her. I told her to run....

The voice-over of Uma reveals the social setup that allows them 'no voice' and extends no compassion:

Uma (voice-over): They knew. Anarkali, Champa and all the *hijra* people knew who are behind the killing of Kamla. They have no voice. The case was hushed up and not even reported in the newspapers. Champa was right. The police made no arrests. Subbu's suicide was written off as an accident. The photograph was destroyed. So were the lives of two young people....

The subjugated mentioned so far from the plays of Dattani are actually psychological studies and the dramatist observes that each one has a common behavioural pattern—search for security and continuous craving for acceptance by the society simultaneously desiring to be true to themselves. Thus, the plays are earnest investigations about socio-cultural authoritarianism and the desire of the trapped individual to be acceptable to the society while remaining true to them.

Works Cited

Chatterjee, Partha. *The Nation and its Fragments.* New Jersey: Princeton University Press, 1993. Print

Dattani, Mahesh. *Final Solutions.* Ed. Angelie Multani. New Delhi: Pencraft International, 2009. Print.

———. *Collected Plays,* Vol. I. New Delhi: Penguin India, 2000. Print.

Goffman, Erving. *The Presentation of Self in Everyday Life.* Edinburgh: University of Edinburgh Social Sciences Research Centre, 1956. Print.

Multani, Angelie, ed. *Mahesh Dattani's Plays: Critical Perspectives.* New Delhi: Pencraft International, New Delhi, 2007. Print.

2

Position of a Man as a Classical Dancer in the Indian Society

Priti Bhatt

Males play a very significant role in Indian classical dance forms that include Kathakali, Kuchipudi, Odissi, and Bhagwath Mela. They were performed only by male dancers in the ancient times.

Tandav was first performed by the God Shiva, Lord of the dance and it is regarded as a male dance. The growth and development of Bharatnatyam was due to the contribution of male teachers. Today, it is one of the most popular Indian classical dance and is practised by male and female dancers all over the world.

There are many renowned classical male dancers in India. Birju Maharaj a maestro of Kathak dance is the head of Lucknow gharana 'school/home of the Kathak Classical Style of northern India'. His solo dance took the form of a demonstration in which he recited complex dance syllables and repeated them on his ankle bells.

In spite of our rich cultural heritage and contribution in the field of dance by men we still can't assure a promising future or recognition to our young boys who want to take dance as their profession or a means of livelihood. In modern twenty-first century also Indian parents would never willingly allow their male child to take Indian Classical dance as a profession.

Tulsi Badrinath, a Chennai based dancer and author of novels like "Man of a Thousand Chances" and "Meeting Lives" learnt Bharatnatyam from a male dancer V.P. Dhananjayan. Her recent book "Master of Arts—A life in dance" is about the difficulties faced by male dancers in the world of Bharatnatyam. She believed men faced prejudice and challenges in learning this art form. She says, "There is this sense of 'who wants to see a man dance' that is particular to Bharatnatyam as compared to other Indian dances."

Indian parents would still prefer their sons to be doctors, engineers or architects etc. than a classical dancer. In our society especially in small towns and cities most of the parents still give more emphasis to academics than learning any art form.

Mahesh Dattani an authentic contemporary playwright, a director, producer and founder of a theatre group known as "Playpen" is an intellectually stimulating Sahitya Akademi Award Winner with an excellent awareness of Indian theatre. In 1998 he won the Sahitya Akademi award for his collection of plays titled *Final Solutions and Other Plays.*

Dattani has boldly explored themes like homosexuality, religious fanaticism, child sexual abuse and gender bias. He also raised the bar for theatrical innovation.

Apart from being a playwright Dattani had another passion to learn dance. With a lot of hesitation in mid-twenties he learnt ballet at the Alliance Francaise run by an English lady. He felt very odd because he barely had a German boy to give him company in the majority girls dance class.

Dattani got inspiration to learn Bharatnatyam dance after seeing the brilliant performance of famous Bharatnatyam dancer Sonal Mansingh. He gave six years of his life in his twenties learning Bharatnatyam. According to him a boy in his twenties learning dance brought forth some sniggers in the society.

After learning this art he realised that Bharatnatyam is an integration of dance, drama and music. He couldn't become a professional dancer but learnt sense of discipline, developed a greater spatial-temporal awareness and understood the richness of Indian Classical tradition. It helped him in learning theatre.

He could understand very clearly relevance among bhava, rasas and rhythm in a drama.

Dattani wrote a remarkable play *Dance Like a Man* while he was learning Bharatnatyam. It's a play that deals with one of his major concerns "gender" through one of his principal passions, dance. This play is about a young man Jairaj wanting to be a dancer but was growing up in a world that believed that dance is for women.

The play *Dance Like a Man* tells us that even men can be at a receiving end of the oppressive power structures of patriarchal society. In our Indian society gender roles are clearly specified for men and women. In this play Jairaj and his wife Ratna want to practise Bharatnatyam in their house but they were living under the domain of Jairaj's father Amritlal who considered dance as a prostitute's profession. According to Amritlal it was improper for his daughter-in-law and absolutely unimaginable for his son.

Dattani expressed the attitude of Indian society of his times when he was young through his play *Dance Like a Man*. Making a reference to the conscience of Amritlal, Asha Kuthari remarks:

> The underlying fear is obvious that dance would make him 'womanly', an effeminate man, with the suggestion of homosexuality, though never explicitly mentioned. This is evident in his plays *Dance Like a Man* as the following quotation suggests.

Amritlal tells his son Jairaj:

> AMRITLAL. "I thought it was just a fancy of yours. I would have made a cricket pitch for you on our lawn if you were interested in cricket. Well, most boys are interested in cricket, my son is interested in dance, I thought. I didn't realize this interest of yours would turn into an....obsession." (Dattani 414)

To her daughter-in-law Amritlal retorts:

> AMRITLAL. "A woman in a man's world may be considered as being progressive. But a man in a woman's world is pathetic." (Dattani 427)

India has become progressive in different areas for example in the field of trade, industries, technology, services, agriculture but still our education system does not have many options for dance courses. The universities in India offer graduation courses in dance and music but they don't assure a promising career prospects for our youths in future.

Another reason for men resenting the image of male dancers is that in our Indian movies many times they are portrayed as weak and effeminate characters. Audience generally ridicule these characters and that has dissuaded young boys from taking this art form.

There are limited opportunities in the present scenario in India for the males who want to choose dance as their career. There are few organisations like "Kartik Fine Arts & Arangham Trust" present "Purush: The Global Dancing Male Conference" in Chennai pursue promises to be an inspired and explosive gathering of diverse artists and scholars. These scholars speak to the audience interested in the male dancing body, history and politics of gender.

The sixty-four-year old Chennai Govt. Music College has opened its doors to male dancers. For centuries devdasis danced in the temples. It's only in the past sixty years that men have performed Bharatnatyam dressed as men.

In Europe there are many well planned graduation courses on dance. They conduct programmes like B.A. (Honours) degree and with this degree students would gain necessary skills to be dance performers, researchers, teachers and choreographers.

These students would get an opportunity to study contemporary and street dance style as well as experiencing African, South East Asian and social dance styles. These programmes also include a compulsory placement module giving students the opportunity to work with dance companies and dance development agencies across London.

To encourage male dancers in our society parents should change their attitude in raising their children. Children should be encouraged to choose their career according to their personal interests. Our young generation should be passionate about their work. The Indian government should suggest our universities to start more systematic courses on non-academics subjects like art, dance, music and painting etc. These courses must be planned in a practical way and students should get compulsory placement opportunities.

According to our Indian society boys should only take interest in academics and painting, dancing or cooking is meant for girls. Our society should not stick to the old gender defined roles set by our ancestors. The government should also take positive and concrete steps in giving due importance to non-academic subjects in our education curriculum. Then parents will take more interest in sending their male child to dance and music schools. An Indian man will proudly learn classical dance provided he gets respect from the society for his talent.

Works Cited

Dattani, Mahesh. *Collected Plays*. New Delhi: Penguin Books, 2000. Print.

———. *Me and My Plays*. New Delhi: Penguin Books, 2014. Print.

———. "Asha Kuthari Chaudhari." 2005. Print.

Kumar, Divya. "Dance Like a Man—A Tribute to Bharatnatyam." *The Hindu*, 17th May, 2013. Print.

Pathmanathan, Subashini. "Male Contribution to Indian Classical Dance." *Daily News*, Srilanka's National Newspaper, 3rd August, 2011. Print.

"Programme Specification for B.A. Urban Dance: Urban Practice." www. Uel.ac.UK/undergraduate/specs/dance.

Srinivas, Ramanujan. "Quality of Teaching is Most Important." *The Times of India*, 8 July 2013. Print.

3

Behavioural Patterns in *Tara*

Shyam Samtani

Going by the primordial myths of creation, Eve was created out of the shoulder ribs of Adam; hence a part of the male persona. Having lavished all his gifts on man, bountiful Brahama borrowed a variety of attributes from nature and invested woman with them to create a companion for him; obviously independent of the male persona. With the passage of time this independent woman was rendered as an inevitable appendage of man, 'never fit for freedom':

> Pita rakshati kaumarya, bharta rakshati youvane
>
> Rakshti sthavire putra, na stri svatantrayam arhati. (Donige 115)

Let alone freedom, she was yoked to the drudgery of domestic duties and reprimanded if she demurred; subjected to verbal and often physical violence too. The miseries multiplied and she was realistically poetized as 'abla nari' with tears as *fait accompli*.

Much water has flown down the Ganges since then and there has been a sea change in the conditions of women all over the world let alone India. With outsourcing in full cry and globalization riding a high tide, India too is reaping rich economic harvest. Multinational companies flap widespread wings. Working in call centres at odd times, the food zones in the sprawling malls are thronged by young girls accompanied by young lads and colleagues. The heavy pay and perquisites have opened new vistas for them. The bars are buzzing with booze and discos with dance to the deafening tune of the DJs. The economic independence is accompanied by liberation from taboos. As regards the success in the corporate sector, women like Indira Nooyi found prestigious place in the 'Women to Watch' published by the *Wall Street Journal*, 2006. The corporate world has Kiran Majumdar Shaw, Chanda Kochar, Nainalal Kidwai, to name a few, at the helm of affairs in India and abroad. Kiran Bedi, Ekta Kapur, Barkha Dutt, Ritu Beri and such others have taken high strides on the ladder of professional/vocational success. But this is true of only a selected segment of society.

It would be a revealing exercise to probe whether this economic progress has changed the psychology of womenfolk and mentality of mankind. What is the lot of the common women at large who are yet to cross over to the other side of the marginalized? Do they have space of their own? Are they still subalterns? Why do we need the warning notice at the diagnostic centres about the sex determination of the foetus being a punishable crime? Do the daughters, as in Tara Patel's 'Mother', still exclaim, "May you never have daughters, mother?" (37). The burning of brides, the dowry persecutions, rapes and gender discriminations abound in news items of everyday life. There have been instances like a woman being chopped and roasted in a tandoor; a two-month old infant being baked in micro oven, reflecting upon the neurotic morbidity of men. Let alone men, even women have connived and been accomplice in the crime or injustice inflicted on their kind. If such a shady deed is done in the family in an open or stealthy manner, how does it affect the behavioural pattern of the family members? What is the impact of the guilt complex on the incumbents and the others who are directly or indirectly, actively or passively, involved in or connected with the unsavory act?

In the back drop of this scenario and the questions agitating the mind, it would be worthwhile to examine Mahesh Dattani's *Tara*, a play dealing with the Siamese Twins, one boy and the other girl.

The play *Tara* occupies a unique, prestigious and prominent place in the entire corpus penned by the playwright Mahesh

Dattani. Erin Mee, the celebrated theatre director and associated with the Department of Theatre in New York University, included "Tara" in her syllabus for a class on Indian Performance. The students responded enthusiastically, writing final papers on this play. "One student pointed out that Tara and Chandan [twin sister-brother] are two sides of the same self rather than two separate entities and that Dan [Chandan renamed in UK], trying to write the story of his own childhood, has to write Tara's story to rediscover the neglected half of himself as a means of becoming whole" (320).

The play revolves round the Siamese twins, Tara and Chandan, their parents Bharati & Patel and Roopa, Tara's friend in the neighbourhood. On his migration to UK Chandan renames himself as Dan. All these characters are on the stage while the twin's maternal grandfather is off staged. On the multi-levelled stage, spot keeps on shifting intermittently to Dr. Thakkar who explains the miracle of physical separation of the pelvic region of the twins as they are conjoined from the chest downwards, a rare feat in the annals of surgery.

At the start of the play, Bharati's behaviour is rather enigmatic. With her husband Patel she is accusative, with her daughter Tara over indulgent, with her son Chandan overt, soliciting with the neighbouring girl Roopa and on the defensive with herself. The pauses and punctuations in her dialogues leave a lot to interpret and make one think if there is any skeleton in the cupboard. Definitely, there is something lurking at the back of her mind—a snake hood trying to pop off but being battened down. The exchange of blemishes between the couple needs reading in between the lines. But like a Robert Frost poem Dattani has the best thought of first though saved for the last. The unexplained digs have taken their toll on all and sundry. In order to straighten the sequence of events and hit the bull's eye it would be meaningful to start from the last, as in the play.

Bharati's father was a top brass politician with far-reaching contacts in Bangalore. After his marriage with Bharati, Patel had to shift there, leaving the parents behind. The wedge is driven deeper after the manipulative interference of the father in the surgical separation of the twins against the medical recommendation, resulting into a disaster. Apart from the other unilateral organs, the twins had just three legs. On thorough investigations, the medical findings were that the blood supply to the third leg was from the girl's body and hence it would remain potent only with her. But the gender construct worked out between the mother and the maternal grandfather (keeping Patel out) and the favours doled out to the surgeon, the third leg was given to the boy. As was suspected, for want of blood supply from the boy's body, the third leg became dead flesh and had to be amputated. Thus, the gender discrimination deprived the daughter of a fair chance for a two-legged existence. Instead, both now have a soft Jaipury leather leg to their social and personal mortification. This secret is not known to the children till late end but it did shroud the mutual relationship of the couple and the two males i.e. Patel and his father-in-law. With this background, it would now be worthwhile to analyze the behavioural patterns of the main characters in the play.

Beginning with the parents, Bharati and Patel, right at the opening, their conversation is tangential, slings and arrows, regarding the use of the gifts left by her late father. The aversion, and so also the rift, is obvious, each trying to camouflage the individual feelings. Representing the upper class mainstream, Bharati and her father favoured the male line by their decision to give the fateful leg to Chandan and thereby deprived Tara of the natural justice. It is pertinent to question how could the mother condescend to such injustice to her own gender or what pushed Patel to such passivity as to remain innocuous. If not taken in confidence during the moment of crucial decision, he could have kept his foot down at the time of actual surgery. Bharati's complicity or Patel's passivity may be a matter of degree but none can be absolved of the guilt. Bharati wilts under the guilt complex and her normal behaviour is adversely affected. She is over protective towards Tara, verbalizing her love, taking pains to convince her that she is more concerned about her than her father:

> Tara! My beautiful baby! You are my most beautiful baby! I love you very much....

> I want you to remember that, Tara....
>
> Everything will be all right. Now that I am giving you a part of me. Everything will be all right....
>
> After the operation, we will all be happy together. And I will make up for...your father, and I will make up for all the things God hasn't given you. (355)

If her behaviour towards Tara is compensatory, it is provocative towards Patel so as to project herself a victim of his male ego and thereby gain sympathy of the children. Gradually she shows signs of neurotic nervousness. Patel shares his anxiety for her health with his neighbour: "May be I'm expecting the worst. It may never happen—no. Things are getting out of hand. I must worry about her. Yes. I am worried about my wife" (330).

Emotionally over strung, she can control neither herself nor the situations. To ensure her behavioural stability Patel insists that she should go to a psychiatrist. When Tara needs a kidney transplant, she offers her own kidney to make good the loss done to her in the past and thereby assuage her guilt. Patel refuses as he has arranged for a donor:

> Bharati: Think of the expenses involved.
>
> Patel: When have expenses ever bothered you? Your father's wealth has always been your strength against me. Don't talk about expenses to me.
>
> Bharati: Why won't you let me do it?
>
> Patel: Because...need I tell you? Because I do not want you to have the satisfaction of doing it.
>
> Bharati: I will do it!
>
> Patel: You will have to obey me. It's my turn now. (344)

The aberrant arguments reach such a feverish pitch that Patel slaps her. Ironically, "the moment she recovers Bharati looks at him with some triumph" (345) as if she has scored a win by pushing Patel to aggression and presenting herself as a marginalized woman, a victim of patriarchy. Her entire behaviour is a calculated move to win her children and convince them of her care, love and indulgence, more than that of their father. It is pity that she was the co-author of the injustice meted out to

Tara, though time and again she verbally demonstrates to the contrary, as a measure of compensatory behaviour. Bharati, who represents the gender construct of the oppressed sex, is partly responsible for the patriarchal preference shown to the male line against the medico-natural laws. Paradoxically, an oppressed oppressor.

Initially Patel found himself helplessly dominated by his father-in-law and his wealth, his wife's strength against him. Subsequently, he picks up the threads and takes control over the situations. He locks his father-in-law's gifts and house admonishing the children to burn rather than use them. He is sympathetic towards Tara and also concerned about Bharati's failing stability. As Tara swoons due to hypoglycemia, while Bharati stands still, unmoved, it is Patel who rushes to bring her sugar and phones up the hospital staff. He tows the patriarchal line for Chandan, his son, who must go to college for higher studies abroad where professionalism has edge over physical handicap. When he finds Chandan staying home and helping Bharati in the feminine activities like knitting, he gets infuriated and sternly warns him to join his office the next day. His approach to the son and daughter is remarkably different. They do not hold any clue to his unrelenting advice that they should visit the ailing mother in hospital only in his presence and not by themselves and the hospital staff too has such orders. This may be unintelligible to Tara but the underlying truth is that Patel does not want the children to hear their mother confessing her guilt and thereby lose their respect for her. His behaviour reflects a dual profile but unfortunately the kids fail to appreciate the real one hidden under the apparent. Whereas the maternal verbose love discernibly floats across, the paternal silent sinks beneath to the chagrin of the offspring, creating a hiatus in the relationship. The consolation comes just towards the end when Dan assures his father during the telephonic conversation, "I never held you responsible for what happened.... How can you feel that it was your fault?" (372). The beguiling behavioural pattern of the parents is thus detrimentally diametric to the real one.

Coming to the siblings, the surgery of the twins is more of emotional than physical separation. The two are complementary to each other. If Tara is sharp and sensitive, Chandan is poetic and inventive. Wit is their forte and laughter their sustenance. They share equal pleasure in music as various symphonies are heard, understood and appreciated. Tara displays feminine susceptibility to her mother whereas Chandan shows masculine assertiveness. He ignores the anxiety caused to his father by his abstinence from physiotherapy. So also the irritability caused by his reluctance to go to college without his sister. Tara is quick to observe the unusual around; be it in person or place and stores it in her armoury for apt use. For example, her observation about Deepa using a rubber sheet on her bed implying that even at thirteen she wets the bed or Roopa having uneven tits. "It's good to know what hurts other people...knowing their secrets is useful" (369). All is fair in self-defense, including Chandan. In case there is any effort to malign or mock any of the twins, she instantly retaliates to nip it in the bud to the embarrassment of the individual. Chandan's sardonic humour is beyond Roopa's intelligence. Their laughter makes her uneasy as she fails to understand the dig. She knows that she is missing the crux of it. The joke is shared between Tara and Chandan at her expense.

Though Tara has matured faster, Chandan's understanding is sounder. Despite Patel's advice not to visit Bharati in the hospital alone, Tara seeks her brother's help to divert Patel's attention so that she can slip into the ward. Chandan declines to help realizing that there must be some reason behind it. They co-exist for each other, completing the incompleteness of the other. After Tara's death, Chandan migrates to UK, renames himself as Dan where he wants to write about his childhood. But instead he ends up writing Tara's. In Tara he finds his other half.

Roopa represents 'the others' in the society, the others with whom there is interaction, who pry, prank, gossip, bicker, create misunderstandings and spread stories. She is 'the ordinary' against whom Tara outshines in her faculties. The behaviour of the physically handicapped is in sharp contrast to that of the mentally imbecile. Her entry and exit reflect upon her ordinary preferences and connections like video watching or carrying her shallow opinion about Bharati or Tara to the other off staged girls. She leads Chandan to sensuality and as his hand slips to her breast, she cries hoarse calling him a 'raper' instead of 'rapist'. She misses the pun of 'peas in a pod', repeating it as 'peas in a pot'. As she hurts Tara and Chandan as ugly freaks, Roopa is cut to size by revelation of Tara's brilliant observation about her uneven tits. In a way even 'the others' in the society are freaks too, though hidden one way or the other. So why fling insults on the natural handicaps by printing posters "we don't want freaks" (378).

Thus, Tara is a thought provoking play with behavioural patterns at different levels of consciousness represented by a guilt ridden mother at pains to redress the wrongs and redeem herself, an innocuously repressed father regaining his patriarchal stature ready to steer the family on to the right track, physically handicapped but mentally agile, bold and brave twins; one witty and the other poetic and the shallow ordinary 'other'.

Works Cited

Donige, Windy (Tr.). *The Laws of Manu.* New Delhi: Penguin Books, 1991. Print.

Patel, Tara. *Single Woman*. Delhi: Rupa & Co., 1991. Print.

Dattani, Mahesh. *Tara* in *Collected Plays*. New Delhi: Penguin Books Pvt. Ltd., India, 2000. Print. (The figures given in brackets are from this source.)

4

Bravely Fought the Queen as Modern Tragedy

Pranav Joshipura

Bravely Fought the Queen is one of the finest plays written in 1991 by India's leading playwright Mahesh Dattani. The play presents a semi-rich urban Gujarati family living in Bangalore. Jiten Trivedi and Nitin Trivedi, the co-owners of an advertising agency, are brothers who have married Dolly and Alka, two sisters. The women usually remain at home and look after their aged mother-in-law, Baa. A couple, Lalitha and Sridhar, has minor role to play. Sridhar is working in the office of the Trivedis as an advertising expert.

The present article is an attempt to analyse tragic intensity in *Bravely Fought the Queen* through women characters it represents and thereby present the tragic vision of Dattani. *Bravely Fought the Queen* is essentially a modern tragedy. Raymond Williams defines modern tragedy as "the life of a man driven back to silence, in an unrewarded working life...men and women broken by the pressure to accept this as normal, and by the deferment and corrosion of hope and desire" (Williams 13). Under such circumstances, the life continues to be lived but there is nothing sort of a joy to impart from this so-called life. The characters in the play, especially the women, are crushed under such pressure and are reverted to silence in a hopeless situation and sacrifice what Hegel defined as their "individual's freedom and independence" (Williams 33). Such a tale presents, in the word of Schopenhauer, "the unspeakable pain, the wail of humanity, the triumph of evil, the scornful mastery of chance, the irretrievable fall of the just and innocent" (Williams 36). Such an effable tale can best be understood through analysis of women characters.

Baa is an almost invalid character who does not die, but has been almost paralytic since then. She had a stroke some time ago. Since then she is bed-ridden. She rings the bell often to call Dolly and Alka. Baa's present is filled only and only with her past memories. She was the daughter of a rich family. It is evident from her delirious utterances in the play that her married life had been painful. Her husband used to beat and abuse her a lot. During one such utterance, she yells out:

> You hit me? I only speak the truth and you hit me? Go on. Hit me again. The children should see what a demon you are. Aah! Jitu! Nitin! Are you watching? See your father! (*Jerks her face as if she's been slapped.*) No! No! Not on the face! What will the neighbours say? Not on the face. I beg you! Hit me but not on...aaaah! (278)

She is not happy with her past and her present seems to be worst looking to her paralytic condition. She is not happy with her sons either. She knows them very well, knows that they are not dependable in anything.

The play suggests that Baa too sang very well. And therefore, the famous singer Naina Devi's life is briefly presented here, to present the contrast of the cruelty of the Trivedi family. Says Dolly,

> She (Naina Devi) married into royalty. Imagine. She could have lived her life comfortably in royal grace and become a rajmata. But she wanted to sing! She wanted to sing songs of love. Thumrissung in her days only by tawaifs. The queen wanted to sing love songs sung by whores! Why? Nobody knew. She'd seen a performance by a tawaif in her youth. The sound of the sarangi and ghungroos remained with her forever. She went ahead and sang! Her husband supported her. At times she was mistaken for a tawaif. But it didn't matter! It didn't matter to her because she was singing! That was all that was important to her. Today, she is called the queen of thumri. (295)

One can see clearly that Baa's husband was the opposite pole of Naina Devi's husband, a mere insensitive brute. Quite possibly there was within her as great a promise as there was in Naina Devi. But her social circumstances did not allow her to realise her potentiality. Human beings are thus the creatures living at the mercy of circumstances. Favourable circumstances can turn a Baa into a Naina Devi and unfavourable ones may reduce a Naina Devi to a Baa. *Bravely Fought the Queen* thus is a tragedy of circumstances in the Indian context where the society is avowedly patriarchal still. Women suffer more and are more helpless than men. Webster's words in this context are equally true that "Woman to man is either a God or a wolf."

Lalitha is reminded of Queen Lakshmi bai when she listens to the story of Naina Devi. But there is apparently no parallel between the two. Lakshmi bai fights and dies. Naina Devi fights with full facilities for fight and lives victoriously. But when Lalitha suggests that Dolly should put on the mask and costume of Lakshmi bai at the proposed ball dance, she does not know, and so also the readers, that how there is a clear parallel between the Queen of Jhansi and Dolly! This is an instance of dramatic irony.

In fact, Dolly seems to be braver than the Queen of Jhansi. The latter fought and fell in the heat of battle. Every soldier dies that way. Courage of hot blood is not as great as the courage of cold blood. Dolly coldly suffers throughout her life with a fortitude no one knows or sings about, in absolute obscurity. Suicide would be more pleasant option to the kind of life she lives. But she prefers to fight until she dies for the well-being of her child. And she is dutiful to her mother-in-law as well. This good woman of a wretched family cannot afford even the luxury of death.

The question is, who is *mardani* Laxmibai, the woman who could be fit to the title of the queen who fights bravely? There are three women whom the title could be applied—Baa, Dolly and Alka. All the three suffer equally bravely. Baa's misfortunes are revealed through her delirious utterances. But she has passed her life. Her past haunts her even in her paralytic wait for the death.

Dolly is an affectionate lady. Circumstances have made her rather dull. The events in the play reveal that her husband is a monster of inhumanity. In Act III, she remembers the unforgettable event. She tells Jiten:

> Fifteen years ago. Hardly married for a year. Praful comes to visit us. The same day, your mother receives a letter from her cousin in Ahmedabad. What fate! It had to be the same day! And it had to be that crucial month for me! What was in that letter? Our whole history. Including the portion which Praful hadn't told you about. (311)

This 'portion' says that Dolly was a child of an illegal union. The revelation angers both Baa and Jiten. The latter under the instigation of the former beats up Dolly badly ignoring rather wilfully that she was pregnant at the time. The result was that the child was born prematurely and had been seriously handicapped. Daksha did not have bones tight enough to hold her straight. Ironically Dolly narrates Daksha's condition to Lalitha this way:

> You want to see her dance? They teach her dance where she goes! Only they call it physiotherapy. I'll bring her tomorrow from her...special school and she will dance for you! Like this....
>
> *She demonstrates a spastic's uncoordinated arm and neck movement with her eyes dilated.* (312)

To her fate of living with a cruel husband and callous mother-in-law was added now the pain of looking after a helpless child entirely dependent upon her mother's care.

But what is Dolly's fault? If she was a good woman before the revelation about her parentage, how would she become bad after that? But customary view refuses to face rationally such simple questions. Dolly is not responsible for her suffering. That is how she is unlike the tragic hero whose misfortunes spring from his character. She is simply the victim of a bad marriage.

Under such circumstances, it is obvious for Dolly to look for some relief. And Dolly finds relief in Kanhaiya, their domestic servant. Two questions arise here: is Kanhaiya a fantasy figure or a reality?

It appears in Act I that Kanhaiya is a real youthful replacement of the cook. Dolly in her suffocation, in her extremely painful situation, needs and deserves a relief. It is quite natural for her under the circumstances to be attracted towards whoever shows affection. So when a young man of Kanhaiya's kind appears on the scene, she may "hit it off" (293) with him. Alka tells us of what she observes of him from her home. Dolly complements her story by saying what happens after the kitchen lights are put off. There seems to be some understanding between Kanhaiya and Dolly that he should come when she plays Naina Devi's *thumri*. The *thumri* is the form of call and Dolly would call Kanhaiya only when her husband and her brother-in-law are away.

But in Act II, there are contrary suggestions. Dolly herself dismisses Kanhaiya as a "half-truth" (293). This means that Kanhaiya may be Dolly's fantasy man. The impulse to have him is genuine. But the event of having had him is fictitious, perhaps. Dattani deliberately maintains the mystery.

Then, there is a suggestion that Kanhaiya as a man does not exist at all. Towards the end of the play, Lalitha asks Dolly:

> I just want to know something. We'll probably never meet again but...I think I know the answer but.... (*Takes a deep breath.*) When I told you Kanhaiya was in kitchen, how did you know I was lying? (*Dolly doesn't respond.*) Tell me. You were so sure I was lying? How? (*No response.*) Oh! I see it all now! I understand! (*Crosses and exits to the kitchen.*) (313)

Lalitha is fully convinced that Kanhaiya does not exist. But it hardly matters whether Kanhaiya is a fact or fantasy. His probability and necessity are patent.

Alka's story is equally tragic. She is a bit more assertive than Dolly. There has been evidence in Act I that her mind revolts against repressive orthodoxy of her family, particularly of Praful. She behaves according to conventions, but also questions conventional ways of behaviour. In Act III, her rushing out in the rain expresses her desire to be free.

Alka is not afraid of anybody. She even dares Jiten. Moreover, she is not afraid of speaking the truth bluntly. She has suffered a lot on account of that. The play presents the fact that as far as she is concerned, her husband is incompetent. However, she probably is unaware about his homosexual reality. She is not able to enjoy a happy family life on that account. Her tragedy is that she is not able to discuss her problem with anyone. To escape from her cold suffering, she gradually resorts to drinking.

Alka tries to present herself as cheerful woman. But that is her outer reality. She in fact hides her personal tragedy beneath her surface. It comes to light at the end of the play in Nitin's soliloquy:

> You (Alka) always were a heavy sleeper. Thank God. Those times when I used to spend the night at your place, I used to sleep on his (Praful's) cot. And he would sleep on a mattress on the floor, beside me.... When all the lights were out, I would lie on the cot. Waiting. For at least an hour.... I would get up and quickly walk to your room.... Yours, your sister's and your mother's. To make sure.... That's right. Don't wake up. Just sleep. And I would go back to Praful's room...and kneel.... At times he would wake up immediately. At other times I would lean forward to look at him. Close enough for my breath to fall gently on his face. And he would open his eyes.... I loved him too. He is...was attractive. And he responded. Oh! But how ashamed he made me feel after! He made me cry each time! That was a game he played. And I-I was caught in it.... He told me to get married.... How could I? And to whom?... He told me that you knew. That he had told you...about me. And that it didn't matter to you. You only wanted the security of a marriage. He...he told me everything would work out fine.... But you didn't know! He tricked you! I-I am sorry. It wasn't my fault. (*Moves to her and slowly covers her face with the blanket.*) But now, you will have to sleep. You mustn't wake up, while I...while I...I mustn't keep him waiting.... (*He moved towards the kitchen.*) The office is not a good idea...too many people passing by...but here–the outhouse. Perfect. Yes. Don't wake up. Stay drunk. You mustn't watch...these powerful arms.... (*Exits to the kitchen.*) (314-15)

Nitin wants her to get drunk and then sleep so that he can enjoy homosexuality with Praful. Alka doesn't know about this reality of Nitin's. But the audience knows. This is another instance of dramatic irony. Alka, like Dolly, also suffers for no fault of her own. She thus is also the queen who fights bravely. In social sense, she is married. But in biological sense, she is not. In a loveless house, she has to pass her time without any satisfaction for her psycho-physiological urges. Is she not the queen who fights bravely?

The sisters have similarities in their suffering. But then there are vital differences in their tales of tears. Dolly has a supporter in Alka who helps, sympathises and understands her problems. But Alka has to suffer silently and all alone. She cannot tell her tragedy to anyone. Praful and Nitin know it and, therefore, they are not very cruel to her. On the other hand, Alka does not have to take care of anyone. She lives alone and will also die alone. She has, thus, the luxury of dying at her will. But Daksha and Baa are dependent on Dolly. Their personal miseries compound Dolly's suffering. Alka's husband is better than Dolly's husband. But is he a husband at all? One does not know whether she is altogether a maiden even after her marriage. May be she has some sexual scratchings now and then. But otherwise she is destined to die an unmarried woman with little experience of man in real sense of the term.

The title *Bravely Fought the Queen* is thus applicable to both. Both fight bravely though their enemies are different and the fields of battle they fight in are not the same. Such tragic tales are never sung by the bards. They sink in oblivion after they cease. Women in India are more or less such sufferers.

One is reminded of Thomas Gray's *Elegy Written in the Country Churchyard*:

> Full many a gem of purest ray serene
> The dark unfathomed caves of ocean bear;
> Full many a flower is born to blush unseen,
> And waste its sweetness on the desert air. (Gray 7)

Moreover, it is interesting to observe that what has happened in the life of Baa is repeating in the life of Dolly. There is an obvious parallelism between two tales of suffering. The play dramatizes two generations and two families of identical nature.

There is one more queen who fights bravely. She is the mother of Praful, Dolly, and Alka. She never appears in the play. The readers do not even know her name. She unknowingly married an already married man. The union had three children thereafter. Her husband then deserted her to live with his former wife. Praful's mother is thus one more victim of man's debauchery. She was, thus, left alone to fend for herself and her three children. In social terms, she is no better than a concubine. Throughout her life, she struggles to keep herself and her children alive under the stigma for no fault of hers. Yet, it appears, she managed to live with dignity. It appears that she had passed away silently before the marriages of Dolly and Alka. Only in details her tragedy is different from that of Dolly, Alka and Baa. All of them are equally the victims of selfish and insensitive husbands in a man-ruled world. The tragedy looks heightened when one sees the lack of sympathy in Baa for a fellow-sufferer, that is, Praful's mother. Does not this nameless creature also deserve the title of the queen who fights bravely?

The play has a character 'The Beggar Woman' who does not play any role in the action. She is only referred to. But, it seems, though outside the action, she reinforces the effect of the whole action with a sort of parallelism. She, too, is a woman. May be the tyrannies not dissimilar to those Dolly and Alka suffer from, had driven her out from her house, driven her to madness. The difference between her and the women in the house of the Trivedies is that she struggles for existence unprotected under wind and rain and changing weather, while the other women have the walls of the house to be within them. That is, they are a bit luckier than she. Is she not the queen who fights more bravely than they?

The above discussion presents women as tragic figures compelled by circumstances of life to lead miserable lives. However, the husbands they are married to are even greater monsters of humanity. A glance at their lives will unfold their types and the kind of tragedy they inflict upon their partners in life.

Jiten, Dolly's husband, is the worst of all the characters. He is full of all the vices, and is greedy and violent, a habitual liar and debauch. Baa says that he is "like his father". He asks Nitin to get rid of Alka to please Baa. On the slightest accusation from Dolly, blaming him for their daughter's condition, he madly rushes out of the house and kills the beggar woman begging beneath a tree by repeatedly running over his car on her.

Nitin is not a monster like Jiten. Act II shows that he is a reasonable person. Money and homosexuality are his two limitations. Nitin wanted Alka to know about his abnormal behaviour before their marriage. But Praful did not tell Alka. Nitin therefore understands Alka's problem and sympathises with her.

Nitin manoeuvres to get Baa's property. Baa does not like Alka and he is prepared to drive Alka out if that would please Baa to make him an heir to property. Nitin hopes that as Daksha is minor, Baa would nominate him as the caretaker of Baa's property till Daksha becomes major. But he is shocked to learn that Baa has not appointed any of the two brothers as the trustee of the property.

Praful turns out to be the most significant character in the play. The technical beauty of the play is that he is not present on the stage. He looked after his sisters after his family was deserted by their father. He got his sisters married. He continues to support them even after their marriage. Thus, Praful emerges as a good person.

Praful is an affectionate person. Baa knows this:

> Look! Look at Praful playing with her (Daksha). My little Daksha! How happy she is with Praful. Look! This is the first time I've seen her smile! She is smiling at Praful! She is trying to get up to go to him! Oh, Praful loves my Daksha! Praful will look after her when I'm gone! (305)

His love for Daksha is genuine. Baa hates him for cheating her. But there is no suggestion in the play of his hate for Baa or Jiten or Nitin. On the contrary, he helps his brothers-in-law by providing them financial assistance.

But why did he lead Alka to marry Nitin despite knowing his private reality? He probably must not have an idea that

Nitin is a confirmed homosexual. Or did he want to continue his homosexual relationship with Nitin through his sister's marriage to him? [One is reminded of Ed in *A Muggy Night in Mumbai* who also had such a plan in thinking of marrying Kiran] Answer to this question is difficult. But the suggestion near the end of the play when Lalitha sees someone climbing the wall in the rain, is clear enough to suggest that the bond of relationship between Nitin and Praful is unbreakable:

> Oh, what's that? The auto driver! He is climbing the wall! Where's he going? To the servants' quarters! (*Spots Sridhar.*) Sridhar! Sridhar, wait! He's gone inside the.... Oh, what's the use? (307)

It is clear that the man climbing the wall is Praful who has secretly come to visit Nitin.

Thus, *Bravely Fought the Queen* provides tragic atmosphere where characters become instruments to events and are played upon cruelly. There is no ending to their suffering and their tale also cannot be narrated in a convincingly logical manner. The women in the play are the heroes, in fact, the tragic heroes who face life squarely and hang on despite unending turmoil in their lives.

Works Cited

Dattani, Mahesh. *Collected Plays*. New Delhi: Penguin Books India, 2000. Print. (The figures in brackets pertaining to the play are from this source).

Gray, Thomas. *Elegy Written in a County Churchyard. Selections in English Poetry*. Delhi: Oxford University Press, 1990. Print.

Williams, Raymond. *Modern Tragedy*. London: Chatto and Windus, 1966. Print.

5

Final Solutions: A Saga of Troubled Legacy

Tausheeh Abbasi

Mahesh Dattani has established himself as a playwright who is said to be the voice of India. His plays are rooted in the reality of the contemporary world and possess a sense of responsibility. Mahesh Dattani's position as a leading dramatist in the Indian English theatre may be attributed to a number of factors. He has created for modern man an image of his urgent concerns. He translates the emotional, social and moral issues of the time into a common language of great power. He is a Realist through and through. Mahesh Dattani has a number of plays to his credit but *Final Solutions* (1993), depicts the societal conditions which have not changed in the last 65 years or to be more precise, since the time of partition of India.

Apparently the main theme of the play is communal hatred and rising fundamentalism in the society but as the plot progresses, it appears that the play is more about prejudices. There is the theme of the oneness of time, the continuity of the past, the present and the future depicting the condition of women in Indian society and the conflict between the modern and the traditional values. Daksha (Hardika), mother of Ramnik Gandhi, exemplifies the past and the present conditions of the women in India. There is a theme of alienation—delineated through Daksha's suffering; the theme of lost identity—exhibited by Javed and Bobby, the Muslim boys; the theme of rise of global thought of oneness exemplified in Smita, Ramnik's daughter; a balance and compromise that Ramnik symbolizes and the theme of faith in religion as shown by the character of Aruna, Ramnik's wife.

The mob and the chorus is symbolic of human hatred and paranoia. They exhibit the reactions of each member of the society as soon as politicians play on their fears and anxieties. People are unable to shake their prejudices and Mahesh Dattani, through the Hindu-Muslim hatred, has depicted the religious hatred and color discrimination, that exists in his world between upper caste and lower caste, whites and blacks, Arabs and Jews. The whole world is facing the problem of rising fundamentalism. It has been rightly remarked: "The demons of communal hatred are not out on the street, they are lurking inside ourselves" (160).

The action in the plot moves between the past situation with Daksha (Hardika) and the present situations with Ramnik, Aruna, Smita, Bobby and Javed. The time varies from 1947 to 1990s. The plot is set in the past in the house of Daksha and in the present in the house of Ramnik Gandhi. The conflict and action oscillates like a pendulum from, between the life of young Daksha, to the life of Smita, her granddaughter. Dattani has created Daksha's character in such a way that she demonstrates the plight of women in India, their oppression and prejudices against religion. Dattani has aptly presented the theme of alienation, as the contemporary age can be rightly called "the age of alienation". The modern man is doomed to suffer the corrosive impact of alienation, which manifests itself variously in the form of the stunning of personal development and the absence of a sense of meaningfulness of life. The contradiction between what the individual aspires for and the harsh reality of what he achieves, what he professes and what he practices, what he really is and what he would like to be taken for has shattered the life leaving a deep effect on his inner being. Taviss suggests:

> Social alienation results from the sense of estrangement brought out by the sudden discovery that the social system is oppressive or incomplete or incompatible with their desires and ideals. The individuals are forced to manipulate in accordance with the social demand or feel incapable of controlling their actions. (Taviss 46-47)

Dattani has skilfully depicted social and self-alienation through Daksha. She is suppressed at home and at her in-law's place. She has no voice of her own. This makes her insecure and her faith in life is lost. She gets prejudiced against religion as her father was killed in the post partition riots. Daksha used to visit her friend Zarine's house, where they listened the gramophone records of Noor Jahan. When communal riots broke off, the shop of Zarine's father was burnt down; Daksha was told that her father-in-law offered a job to Zarine's father, which he turned down. Daksha was filled with hatred for Muslims and a kind of depression engulfed her. Dattani has beautifully portrayed the time shift from Daksha's past to Hardika's present:

> Hardika. After forty years...I opened my diary again. And I wrote. A dozen pages before. A dozen pages now. A young girl's childish scribble. An old woman's shaky scrawl. Yes, things have not changed that much. (167)

Mahesh Dattani portrays women characters and their fantasies very candidly as he tells in an interview that he believes that he can forget his own gender, so that the scenes between women do come from the outside view point at all. Women have not been presented as sinners, but they suffer because of the society and men who are part of their lives. Psychological activity is a complex of aggressive and defence mechanism whose final purposes is to guarantee the continued existence of the organism and to enable it to develop in safety. Psychological activity cannot be imagined in isolation. The reactions of Daksha, Ramnik, Javed, Bobby and Smita can be understood clearly, in their relation to their environment, receiving and responding to stimuli from outside. All of them are grappling on the one hand with the changed realities of Indians life since independence and the trauma they entail, on the other hand with their psychic conflict of personal origin.

Freud gives three tier structures of personality—Id, ego and super ego and they may be treated as representatives respectively of the body, mind and society in the psychic structure of men. If the balance amongst these three is disturbed, a crisis becomes inevitable and an individual has to resort to defence mechanism. If the individual has to put up with an excess amount of repression, the defence mechanism fails and the situation becomes ripe for the onset of neurosis. According to Freud: "In the conflict between the desires and sense of duty, she once more seeks refuge in a neurosis" (Freud 61).

Daksha, Javed and Bobby are forced to kill their basic instincts and have to succumb to the wishes of the society. Carl Jung's theory of personal unconscious is quite similar to Freud's creation of a region containing a persons repressed, forgotten or ignored layer of the collective unconscious. It is a storehouse of talent, memory traces inherited from man's past. The environment has a deep impact on shaping man's collective unconscious. Carl Jung said: "The individual is increasingly deprived of the decision as to how he should live his own life, and instead is ruled, fed, clothed and educated as a social unit" (Jung 247).

Daksha has lots of the latent memories of the past that affect her personality on which the personal unconscious and the ego are built. The collective unconscious makes her hostile towards a particular community. Daksha/Hardika stays with her son Ramnik who is a liberal, secular man and is free from any kind of prejudices against religion. He believes in harmony, peace and compromise. The tension in the plot rises when communal riots start in Ramnik's town during a Rath Yatra as someone pelted stones, the wheel of the chariot broke down and the idol fell on the ground. The Chorus depicts the feelings of the Hindus and Muslims;

> The Muslim Chorus: We are neither idol makers nor breakers why did they blame us.
>
> The Hindu Chorus: This is our land. It is in their blood to destroy. (167)

Ramnik gives shelter to two Muslim boys, Bobby and Javed against the wishes of Hardika and Aruna, his wife. Mahesh Dattani, through the theme of religious prejudices, compels us to wonder, what we are going to get out of these ill feelings for one another. It shatters the faith, the inner psyche and increases socio-cultural imbalance. The political intervention in Indian society is so powerful that it creates havoc in the social life of the people. The politicians, who are the caretakers of the nation, take care of their own selfish motives, from behind the mask of secularism. The chorus in the play gives the notion, when they feel that their cries and hatred are meaningless: "Chorus 1. There is heartache. We doubt the leader's intentions. They want our blood to boil. They have succeeded" (188).

Mahesh Dattani has tried to establish the idea that the feeling of insecurity can be a cause for rising prejudices and fundamentalisms. The customs and beliefs of the society sometimes have a negative influence on the psyche of a person. Bobby gives the reason how a minor incident changed Javed from a hero of the school to an extremist. It happened when the boys were playing cricket and the postman asked Javed to hand over the letter to the neighbor. Javed did it and kept the letter on the wall, the neighbor came out, wiped the letter and the spot as a Muslim had touched them. Javed reacted and threw meat and bones into his backyard. Javed and Bobby represent the theme of lost identity. They face an acute sense of alienation and a sense of dislocation from the mainstream. The reactions were different. Javed became an extremist and Bobby was ashamed of himself.

> Bobby. Yes like being apologetic. For being who I was. And pretending that I was not a part of my community. For thinking that I could become superior by not belonging. Nobody called me Baboon in College. I chose to be called Bobby. (201)

When Ramnik decides to handover Javed to the police he reveals the truth that the riots are systematically planned and organized in such a manner that the real culprits lie hidden and they provoke the feelings and religious sensitivity of innocent people. Javed says:

> Javed. The first screams are of sensing an unusual freedom. And suddenly you come crashing down, and you want to get off. You scream with pain and horror. Everyone is along in their own cycles of joys and terrors. Why am I here? What am I doing here? The joyrides get over. It is a terrible feeling. Being disillusioned. (205)

Mahesh Dattani has portrayed the conflict between modern values and traditional values as represented by Smita and Aruna respectively. The Indian element is given by Dattani when

Aruna talks of Sanskars and how one should be proud of one's inheritance. But Smita says that she has no faith in religion. Smita is prejudiced about religion. She respects her parents but she is not ready to learn the preaching of her mother. She asks her mother why she should feel insecure with the two boys if she has faith in God. Smita and Bobby loved each other but now they have followed different paths. Aruna asks Smita to fill the brass pot with water for her pooja; Smita, Javed and Bobby move out to get water. Smita asks Javed to touch the pot and fill it. Dattani perhaps wants to give the idea that all religions move in one direction. Bobby takes up a bold step by moving towards the pooja room and picking up Lord Krishna's idol.

> Bobby. Look how He rests in my hands! He knows I cannot harm Him. He knows His strength! I don't believe in Him but He believes in me. He smiles at our trivial pride and our trivial shame. You can bathe Him day and night, you can splash holy waters on Him but you cannot remove my touch from His form. You cannot remove my smell with sandal pastes and attars and fragrant flowers because it belongs to a human being who believes, and tolerates, and respects what other human beings believe. That is the strongest fragrance in the world. (223-24)

Communal attitudes are deeply embedded within the characters and they are prejudiced against each other's religion. But Mahesh Dattani successfully shows a ray of hope by shaking our conscience and making us aware of the reality of communal violence. Dattani suggests that religious fervor emanates from perceptions of being wronged and degrades to actions of doing wrong. The plot is a complex one, encompassing a number of subplots, conflicts, yet maintaining the unity and giving a final impression. The final revelation by Ramnik to Hardika that the shop of Zarine's was destroyed and burnt by her husband and father-in-law, as they wanted a shop in that place, the shop is now owned by Ramnik. He tells Hardika that "They are not the only one who have destroyed" (226). Hardika is crushed and filled with guilt and shame. She asks Ramnik, "Will the boys ever come back?" (226).

The play has a bold theme but it spreads the message of believing in one another. Perhaps the final solution lies in our inner selves when we have to conquer our prejudices and then nothing can destroy us. The play involves a lot of introspection not only on the part of the characters but also on the part of the readers. When asked if he was upset to see the problems—social, political or unconventional, Dattani says,

> They invariably do. Social issues move me and I like to examine an idea from different angles. The plays where the content came first are *On a Muggy Night* and *Final Solutions*. As for the latter, I was asked to write a play about communal tensions and I said, 'what can one write about that other than platitudes'? But out of that churning emerged *Final Solutions*.

Works Cited

Dattani, Mahesh. "Final Solutions." *Collected Plays*. New Delhi: Penguin Books, 2000. Print. (Figures in brackets are from this source.)

Freud, Sigmund. *On Psychopathology, Inhibitions Symptoms and Anxiety.* London: Penguin Books, 1979. Print.

Jung, Carl. *Memories, Dreams and Reflections*, Vol. 10, ed. Aniela Jaffe, London: Routledge, 1962. Print.

Taviss, I. "Changes in the Form of Alienation." *American Sociological Review*, 34/ 1 Feb. 1969. Print.

6

Rituals and Cultural Idioms in Urban Context: A Critical Reflection of Mahesh Dattani

Nisha Tiwari

Mahesh Dattani is one of the most prolific contemporary Indian playwrights in English whose plays engage with the crises of urban existence and the elite upper middle class section of the Indian society. His target audience, therefore, is a slice of the Indian population mostly comprising of the urban masses. In an interview regarding the urban contexts of his plays, Dattani states, "I think there are enough issues and challenges in urban Indian society (the milieu that I am part of) and these automatically form the content of my work" (Mee 19). His plays often grapple with issues of modernity, liberal education, traditional identity, *et al.* In order to deal with the conglomeration of these issues that have an overlapping significance for the upper middle class of the urban India, Dattani interweaves his drama with narratives of rituals and ritualistic traditions. This paper studies Dattani's use of cultural idioms of ritual as an instrument for exposition of the incongruities of the urban socio-cultural structures that deploy the rituals against those marginalized communities whom these ritualistic narratives serve to accommodate and express. In the context of modern Indian theatre, the paper will take into consideration the following three plays: *Dance Like a Man* (1989), *Seven Steps Around the Fire* (1998) and *Thirty Days in September* (2001) for their use of rituals in order to contest the heterosexual androcentric tradition of the patriarch which they are supposed to celebrate.

Catherine Bell enumerates three contexts in which "ritual" and its process ought to be understood. First, "historical dimension"—where a certain act or code of conduct is passed on as tradition from one generation to the next; second, "regional" dimension, involving "domestic to national" logistics; and, third, "organizational", i.e. encoding a certain code of conduct into the lived experience as the standard (118). She further opines that "ritual" is not a fixed entity; rather, it is eternally in flux, which also becomes sites of negotiation and process of legitimization. It is dynamism of the phenomenon of the ritual that the playwright in question taps on to in order to flesh out the conflict in his plays. Dattani interweaves these dimensions into the narratives of rituals amidst which his characters are shown to negotiate their personal and social destinies. His plays deploy these narratives, be it of Bharat Natyam and the devadasis (*Dance Like a Man*), *hijra* and Hindu wedding rituals (*Seven Steps Around the Fire*) and Bhakti and its dictates of submission and protection for the Bhakta (*Thirty Days in September*). In each case, the conflict lies in the characters' struggles against the ritual and the social structures that these legitimize. The playwright under scribes the issue of identity—personal, social and national that Bell mentions—amidst this crisis while engaging in a semiotic encoding and decoding of the same with the help of rituals.

The protagonist Jairaj, in the play *Dance Like a Man,* struggles to escape from his father's persistent dominance even after the latter's death. Amrutlal was a modern, liberal thinker during India's freedom struggle, working for the upliftment of the marginalized. His liberal thinking is put to test when he sees his son pursuing Bharatnatyam. By using the narrative of dance, the play hits at the incongruity of the oppressive heterosexual and androcentric normative social order of the post-Independence "modern" India of which Amrutlal Shah is a prototype. He is an upper-class liberal freedom fighter who thinks that while preserving cultural heritage deserves respect, the subjects/victims of the cultural tradition do not deserve much attention, "Gaining Independence was a part of our goal. And someone has to be in charge. It's what we do not that counts. As you know, our priority is to eradicate certain unwanted and ugly practices [viz., Bharatnatyam and Devadasis] which are shame to our society.... I will not have our temples turned into brothels" (*Dance* 416). Amrutlal's idea of nation and patriotism lies in the heterosexual androcentric worldview of organized and clean cities with temples and monuments as symbols of rich cultural heritage. Through the cultural idiom of the patriarch, represented in Amrutlal's character, Dattani contests the notion of freedom, and the logistics of lived freedom in post-Independence India where the androcentric definitions of the same are the norm.

Amrutlal's hostility towards the profession does not stem only from the "underbelly" of Bharatnatyam—for ultimately he does allow his daughter-in-law Ratna to pursue it. However, the traditional rhetoric sees devadasis dancing to celebrate God, the prototypical male. The mere thought of his son, trying to dance like girls to celebrate the male, was acceptable till he was a young boy, but not now when he is a man. The possibility of this threatens Amrutlal's notions of masculinity,

> Amrutlal: I have never seen a man with long hair.
>
> Jairaj: All sadhus have long hair.
>
> Amrutlal: I don't mean men. I mean normal men.... I have noticed the way he walks.
>
> (*Dance* 417)

The patriarch that he is, Amrutlal does not allow his heir the freedom to experiment with any alternate definition of a man besides the heteronormative one even if it pushes the latter towards alcohol. "...[he] would sooner watch me turn into a drunkard than see me dance" (*Dance* 444) observes Jairaj. Jairaj's refusal to "grow up into an adult" is a pronounced gesture of rebellion. According to Mithran Devanesen, "The younger Jairaj tries to go against this ["the autocratic father" and the "unwritten rules of authority"] in the play that examines authority and prejudice socially and culturally and as...the story unfold[s] between time past and time present, Mahesh Dattani forces us to examine our own individual and collective consciousness" (*Dance* 383). Jairaj resists being turned into another male who inherits the reins of an oppressive patriarch. It is curious to see that it is Ratna, Jairaj's wife, who takes on this position of authority in the family after Amrutlal's death, forcing their daughter Lata to "grow into an adult". It is not a matter of coincidence that Ratna feels threatened by Lata's success, since she sees it as a threat to her own reputation, in the manner that Amrutlal sees Jairaj as a threat.

While Dattani shows that the Indian familial space refuses to give up its celebration of the head/the patriarch, he also delicately introduces possibilities of change. To this purpose, Dattani uses a variety of cultural markers. The traditional house, the brocade shawl, and the rocking chair are all signifiers, both cultural and metaphoric, of Amrutlal Parekh's presence looming large. At the same time, the "extended drawing room" (that Jairaj built over his father's garden), Jairaj's ghungroo, which Lata wore to her first dance performance, and Jairaj's hidden bottle of whisky are signifiers of resistance and change. Dattani portrays a different figure of a father in Jairaj who lets his daughter pursue her dreams and also marry the man she wishes to marry. It is no coincidence that their son Shankar is shown to have died at an early age, thus also ending any threat of the return of the patriarch had he grown into an "adult". The play ends with Jairaj moving out of the house, and pursuing his dance even after his father's death, thus, being liberated from the pressures of the family tradition that had ruined his lived experience.

In fact, the title of the play, *Dance Like a Man*, itself manifests the crisis most articulately. It projects the ritual and social systems as a paradox. While dance, in this case Bharatnatyam, is the dance of the Gods, ritually also believed to be performed by them, its social practice is restricted to women. To be able to dance "like a man" would culturally mean to be able to be absolutely brave and apologetic about it. The play, as the audience sees, revolves around Jairaj's struggle to acquire and inhabit a time and space that allows him to dance like a man. It allows one to witness how rituals of patriarchy are repressive even to men who are forced to 'perform' the rituals of masculinity.

Dattani incorporates into his texts other cultural idioms and rituals that have been bolstering the patriarchy for ages, only to use them as a touchstone to test the veracity of post-independent Indian framework of values, liberalism, modernity and tradition. His in-depth use of rituals and their conceptual paradigms help the audience to assess their significance in the contemporary social space. As Mary Douglas opines that ritual is an activity in which the personal and the social bodies mutually constitute each other (qtd. in Shepherd *et al.* 121). On the other hand, Bell argues that ritualization is essentially a repetition of the basic binary opposition with the aim to naturalize it (102). The prevalent binary structures in the Indian culture are those of gender and sexuality, which the playwright deploys time and again. Dattani's play, *Seven Steps Around the Fire*, celebrates the patriarch—its heterosexual normativity—in the figures of the Minister Sharma, DCP Rao, and the protagonist Uma's husband, Suresh Rao, the Chief Superintendent of Police, who successfully restores law and order amidst the temporary threat brought upon the heterosexual normative order by the *hijra* community of the city of Bangalore. They silence the scandal of the murder of Kamala, a *hijra*, by Minister Sharma for marrying his son, Subbu. Subbu's death is a voluntary act in response to Kamla's loss, whereas Kamla's death is a punishment meted out for her transgression. Kanika Batra argues, "Dattani's conceptualization of the nation-state foregrounds the political edge of the representation of sexuality.... [It] is political indictment that holds the state accountable for failing to protect the social, economic and legal rights of minorities marked by their caste, gender and sexuality" (96). Uma's thesis explores the class-gender-based power implications around the *hijra* community in India, which also forms the backdrop to this play. The sociological details of the cultural significance of the *hijras* features as a part of Uma's research recordings, which features time to time in the play, "Perceived as the lowest of the low, they yearn for family and love. The two events in mainstream Hindu culture where their presence is acceptable—marriage and birth—ironically are the very same privileges denied to them by man and nature" (*Seven* 11).

Dattani portrays the acute homophobic character of the androcentric Hindu culture. Suresh and Munswamy, the constable, and Minister Sharma, constantly refer to Anarkali, a *hijra*, as "it", unable to accord Anarkali a pronoun as it threatens to destabilize the sacrosanct socio-cultural framework which is premised upon the binary opposition of gender, therefore, also threatening their self-assurance regarding their own masculinities. Suresh vehemently states, "They are all just castrated degenerate men" (*Seven* 10). It is, therefore, easy to understand why Suresh refuses to be tested for fertility, since his idea of masculinity is deeply entrenched to this aspect. The sexual sterility is only for the *hijras* as in opposition to his "masculine" identity. Kanika Batra recognizes Dattani's "commitment to present unrecognized and stigmatized forms of domesticity, sexuality, and productivity... [and] present alternative sexual arrangements reliant on ritualistic gendered and sexual labor including heterosexual and homosexual prostitution, performances by *hijras* on occasions such as the birth of a child or a wedding in the family..." (93). In this respect, Anarkali's sexual abuse can be seen as an extortion, through sexual labour, as a price to be paid for her intrusion into the social space, even if it is the jail.

To an extent, Uma's own intent to help the *hijras* stems from her anxiety about the curse, which according to her foster mother, was the reason that the latter had not been able to reproduce. Her advice to the minister to allow *hijras* to bless the heterosexual alliance of Subbu and his wife, and the latter's acquiescence to the same, stems from their cultural consciousness of the power of the curse of infertility. The *hijras* are seen to be an unnecessary traditional intrusion into the otherwise sacrosanct heterosexual space of the social order. The sexual sterility of Subbu's heterosexual marriage and that of Uma and Suresh runs parallel to the accounts of violence meted out to the *hijras* on account of their sexual sterility. Dattani destabilizes this axiom with Champa, the matriarch of the *hijra* community, blessing Uma with the possibility of children. Nevertheless, the deliberate silencing of Kamala's murder case and reasons for Subbu's suicide with the annexation of the wedding photograph of Subbu and Kamla, allows the heterosexual normative order to continue its course as smoothly as before. Dattani exposes the stifling liberalism of the upper class androcentric view that silences anyone who threatens their position—even if it is one's own son.

Thirty Days in September also encodes this continuum of the patriarch through the silence of the victims of sexual abuse, both mother Shanta and daughter Mala by the same man, Shanta's eldest brother Vinay. Dattani uses the same character, calling him "the Man", to play different men that Mala tries to have a sexual relationship with, to underline the experience of sexual and emotional anxiety that she undergoes throughout her life due to the childhood trauma. He also represents himself as "the Man" of the Khatri household, which privileges him with the right to act as Mala's father to approve her alliance with Deepak. The playwright tries to manifest the panoptical God-like presence of the patriarch as an instrument to regulate and subjugate the female agency and sexuality. Mala exclaims, "I see this man [Vinay] everywhere. I can never be free of him. I am not sure whether I have the ability to love anyone...else" (*Thirty* 54).

As the name suggests Shanta is shown to be a docile, silent housewife, who much to the despair and ire of her daughter, keeps herself busy in the puja room worshipping Krishna. The mother shares a dysfunctional relationship because of Shanta's silence over her daughter's sexual abuse, until Shanta breaks her silence revealing her own experience of being abused by Vinay, "I remained silent not because I wanted to, but I didn't know how to speak.... I looked to Him [God]. I didn't feel anything. I didn't feel pain, I didn't feel pleasure. I lost myself in Him" (*Thirty* 55). In this respect her bhakti is not an act of absolution, as much an act of release. Her silence, which she later eternalizes by slicing her tongue, is an act of defiance manifested in a refusal to speak in a world of those blind to her pain—her brothers, parents and also her own daughter. This world is one where, "Only he [Vinay] spoke. Only he said, only he saw and he did" (*Thirty* 55). In each case, be it Mala or Shanta, as Dattani remarks, "It is the silence that makes the abused feel betrayed" (qtd. in Sonker 2). Dattani sees silence as an important ingredient in the construction of the Indian family and social framework, where silence is a great virtue of the Indian family. He comments, "It's the silence and the betrayal of the family that affects me the most" (qtd. in Sonker 2). Silence, in his plays, becomes an aesthetic tool to not only build suspense but also as a device of exposition when the normative order is destabilized temporarily to allow to audience to absorb the enormity of the cultural crisis that is laid bare before them. Thus silence becomes a strong agency for social and individual expression in the play, as opposed to its perception as a sign of submission and surrender.

Dattani skilfully provides the backdrop of the bhakti ritual, its silence and submission to throw light on the helplessness and surrender of the sexual victim to the Man. Shanta is always seen ringing a bell and singing, "Mere to Giridhar Gopal doosro na koi," where the song reveals Shanta's condition, and the bell, which rings till the end of the play, further resounds with telling tale of sexual violence immersed in Shanta's silence of a lifetime.

As witnessed in the discussion of these plays, Dattani taps into the cultural and ritualistic rhetoric and practices only to unearth the voices suppressed by them. In each of these plays, Dattani deliberately leaves his audience with a sense of uneasiness and a perturbed conscience. In an interview with Anita Nair, Dattani states "You can't treat a play like a roller coaster ride which even at its most terrifying moment you know will end soon and quite happily when you hit terra firma. It's only when you are left hanging in air you start to question your own personality, perceptions etc. Like I said before, the theatre is a collective experience and the audience have to finish in their own heads what the playwright began" (Web Link). While he borrows his penchant for shocking realism from Western theatre, his use of the ritual and cultural allows his theatre to indigenize itself to the needs of the urban Indian audience.

Dattani deals with the issues that, according to Aparna Dharwadekar, occupy the contemporary Indian theatre scene, viz., the intensely problematic relation of such concepts as modernity, contemporaneity, and postcoloniality to drama, theatre, and performance in present-day India" (2). By using the English language and the urban space, the playwright includes the postcolonial voice and struggle with modernity, at the same time also placing under the lens, the collective cultural consciousness that his Indian audience has acquired over generations and struggles with every day to define its own situation in contemporary India.

Works Cited

Batra, Kanika. “Queering the Subaltern: Postcolonial Performativity in Mahesh Dattani’s *Seven Steps Around the Fire* and Mahasweta Devi and Usha Ganguli’s *Rudali.*” *Feminist Visions and Queer Futures in Postcolonial Drama: Community, Kinship, and Citizenship*. New York: Routledge, 2011: 92-110. Print.

Bell, Catherine. “Ritual Tradition and Systems.” *Ritual Theory, Ritual Practice*. New York: OUP, 1992: 118-42. Print.

Dattani, Mahesh. “Seven Steps around the Fire.” *Mahesh Dattani: Collected Plays*. New Delhi: Penguin, 2000: 1-42. Print.

———. “Dance Like a Man.” *Mahesh Dattani: Collected Plays*. New Delhi: Penguin, 2000: 381-448. Print.

———. “Thirty Days in September.” *Mahesh Dattani: Collected Plays*. Vol. 2. New Delhi: Penguin, 2005: 1-58. Print.

Dharwadekar, Aparna. “Postcolonial Frames and the Subject of Modern Indian Theatre.” *Theatres of Independence: Drama, Theory, and Urban Performance in India Since 1947*. Iowa City: U of Iowa, 2005: 1-18. Print.

Mee, Erin. “Mahesh Dattani: Invisible Issues.” *Performing Arts Journal* 19, (Jan. 1997): 19-26 Print.

Nair, Anita. “Mahesh Dattani: The Invisible Observer.” 31 Jan. 2014. <http://www.anitanair.net/profiles/profile-mahesh-dattani.htm>.

Shepherd, Simon and Mick Wallis. “Performance Studies: Some Basic Concepts.” *Drama/Theatre/Performance*. New York: Routledge, 2004: 116-33. Print.

Sonker, Santosh Kumar. “Mahesh Dattani’s Thirty Days in September: A Study in the Treatment of Incest.” 1 Feb. 2014. <http://www.the-criterion.com/V2/n3/Santosh.pdf>.

7

Mahesh Dattani: The Face of Modern Indian Drama in English

Deepa Diddi

The post-modern era has been productive for Indian English Drama as it has received fresh impetus from young writers like Mahesh Dattani and Manjula Padmanabham. They have infused new life into drama by projecting stark realism through their plays. Recent years have witnessed a spurt of the Indian drama in regional language. Extensive translations of regional plays into English have established a bond between East and West, North and South.

Mahesh Dattani is one of India's most daring and innovative playwrights writing in English today. He blends conventional themes with startlingly new ones in his work. His plays combine the intimate with the social, the personal with the public, often exploring the boundaries between these realms. In 1998, Mahesh Dattani became the first Indian playwright in English to be awarded the Sahitya Akademi Award for his collection titled *Final Solutions and Other Plays*. The success of Indian playwrights like Mahesh Dattani is significant because unlike the Indian novel and Indian poetry in English, Indian drama in English does not have a long and enabling tradition. In spite of the rich and varied tradition of Sanskrit drama, the Parsi theatre, and drama in other Indian languages, there is very little Indian drama in English. There are of course a few, such as Asif Currimbhoy, Nissim Ezekiel, Gurucharan Das, Dina Mehta, and

Pratap Sharma who have given us some good plays. But these plays have had a very limited appeal and were more often read than performed on stage. In contrast, more people have seen Mahesh Dattani's plays on stage than read them.

Dattani chooses expressionism to illustrate the continuous struggle of the contemporary urban Indian in familial, social and cultural spheres to create his individual identity. This struggle is the subject of almost all his plays. Expressionism as a technique presents, "what life is like when the external pretences are dropped". Since the plays display distorted modern man's psyche on the stage, the stage and its settings are divided into different levels. To present psychological realism, apart from multilevel sets, various symbols and symbolic devices are used and the setting is purposefully made of unfamiliar pieces. The time sequence is highly disturbed to show the troubled and frustrated human psyche. The plot, thus, often moves forward and backward to illustrate a considerable time on the stage.

Dattani, an adept playwright and theatre practitioner, finds the issue and creates characters, simultaneously uses the stage, space and time that suit the subject he treats. The characters on the stage are contemporary urban Indians. The issues they deal with are socio-cultural conflicts; about the marginalised sections of our society: minorities, women, gays, and eunuchs. They expose the violence of our private thoughts, and the hypocrisy of our public morals.

Dattani is a trend setter, dealing with the issues of the marginalized in the Indian urban society. *On a Muggy Night in Mumbai* is the "first play in Indian theatre to handle openly gay themes of love, partnership, trust and betrayal" (John 45). *On a Muggy Night in Mumbai* is also adapted as film entitled Mango Soufflé. Both the play and the film describe the issue of the same sex love. Though, there are different locales of both the play and the film, the theme, the characters, the events etc. are same in both the works. The film Mango Soufflé is a daring attempt to unmask the gay-relationship veiled under the domination of heterosexuals' relationship of society that considers it as a disgusting, unnatural, and undesirable.

The play takes us through the lives of Kamlesh, Ed, Bunny, Prakash, Sharad, Deepali and Kiran. They are homosexuals who are trying to create a space for themselves by asserting their own ideology, flamboyancy and rejection of traditional approach. *On a Muggy Night in Mumbai* is a play about the travails of gay men and women, some of them strongly anti-heterosexual.

In the play, Prakash and Kamlesh were deeply in love with each other. The separation between the two causes immense pain and distress to Kamlesh. He then comes in contact with Sharad and a gay relationship develops between them. Kamlesh, however, is unable to adjust with Sharad, as he is haunted by the memories of Prakash.

It comes as a great shock to him, that Prakash has changed his name to Ed, and intends to marry his divorcee sister, Kiran. He invites his friends, in order to find a solution for his problem. Kamlesh asks his friends to help him forget Prakash.

> I came here to get over a relationship.... As gay men and women, we have all been through that,... I did a cruel thing by loving Sharad to forget Prakash. I have not succeeded.... I made Sharad go through the same pain and suffering that I was trying to get over.... Please! I am afraid! I need your help! (67-68)

Dattani brings to the fore the crisis that gays face as they are torn between their true self and what the traditional Indian society thinks and expects of the gays. Their hidden fears and feelings are carefully portrayed in the play. Dattani, within the framework of dramatic structure, tries to investigate the identity crisis of the gays who do not get a respectable space in society. Their issue is considered a taboo and is brushed under the carpet. *On a Muggy Night in Mumbai* is a play that depicts the social space of violence and humiliation faced by them. First performed at the Tata Theatre, Mumbai on 23rd Nov., 1998 *On a Muggy Night in Mumbai* is probably the best and the most complex play that discusses the socio-psychological identity crisis of gays who are torn between the social taboos and their personal desires, their conscience and social consciousness. It dramatizes the conflicts, anguish, dilemmas, insecurities, fears and frustration of the gays in the society. John McRae comments:

> It is not simply the first play in Indian theatre to handle openly gay themes of love, partnership, trust and betrayal. It is a play about how society creates patterns of behaviour and how easy it is for individuals to fall victim to the expectations society creates. (John 45)

We meet a host of gays at Kamlesh's party in his flat and they represent the varied faces of the homosexual community. They all are complex characters who cannot be understood by their outward gender preferences alone. They have their own fears and fantasies, cares and concerns, conscience and consciousness, emotions and passions as part of their personality traits, like anybody else. They have different expressions regarding their identity. They have gathered together at the invitation of Kamlesh who is a 'recluse' in the heart of Bombay and is unable to forget his lover Ed/Prakash. Kamlesh shares his agony at being betrayed by Prakash/Ed with the group:

> I would have understood it if he had left me for another man, but he left me because he was ashamed of our relationship. It would have worked between us, but he was ashamed. (68-69)

Kamlesh does not want to hide his true self. He says, "How long shall we continue to hide? We can't hide forever!" (91). But his gay partner, Ed, has betrayed him and he feels down and out because of that. "For the first time in my life, I wished I wasn't gay" (69). He even tries to take the help of a psychiatrist out of the 'Yellow Pages' who pretends to understand his case and tells him about the 'aversion therapy' to help him fight the depression but "He said I would never be happy as a gay man. It is impossible to change the society, he said, but it may be possible for you to reorient yourself" (69). Heterosexual society, Dattani suggests, wants everyone to repeat the stylised acts it sanctions. Kamlesh brings out the stark reality:

> I tried explaining to him that I needed his help to overcome my anxiety and fear not to be something I am not. Could

> he help me cope my loneliness and fear the same way he would help a heterosexual cope with his? (69)

Kamlesh is not able to cope with the loneliness and becomes more obsessed with the memory of Ed. He ends up "picking up strangers-bringing them over-hoping to connect" (70). He indulges in sexual relations with the guard and the secretary of the society as well. It is the failure on the part of Kamlesh to 'reorient' but success or at least a pretension of success on the part of Ed when he pretends to be 'straight' because the church and the psychiatrist have helped him believe that his love for Kamlesh was "the work of the devil. Now the devil has left him" (85). It is not the individuals alone who disapprove homosexuality but the high institutions of society like church which do not approve and sanctify such relations because relations between same sex, since they cannot be procreative are seen as unnatural and carnal.

Ed leaves Kamlesh because he wants to hide his gay identity and decides to marry Kiran to become socially acceptable. He actually wants to remain in touch with Kamlesh through Kiran so that nobody suspects his identity. He says, "Nobody would know. Nobody would care...I'll take care of Kiran. And you take care of me" (105). He sees no future in open gay relationship. He does not want himself to be branded publically as a gay. He defends himself of his intentions of pretending 'straight', when he says,

> Look around you. Look outside.... There are real men and women out there. You have to see them to know what I mean. But you don't want to. You don't want to look at the world outside this—this den of yours. All of you want to live in your own little bubble. (99)

The play revolves around the identity crisis in the life of all the gays, like Ed. Bunny Singh, another example in the play, admits that he is just trying to "Camouflage...Blend with the surroundings!" (70). Sharad tells Kiran why gays try to hide their identity:

> You see, being a heterosexual man—a real man, as Ed put it—I get everything. I get to be accepted—accepted by whom?..well, that marriage lot down there for instance.

> I can have a wife, I can have children who will all adore me simply because I am a hetero—I beg your pardon—a real man. Now why would I want to give it all up?

So what if I have to change a little? If I can be a real man I can be king. Look at all the kings around you, look at all the male power they enjoy, thrusting themselves on to the world, all that penis power! Power with sex, power with muscle, power with size. Firing rockets, exploding nuclear bombs, if you can do it five times I can do it six times and all that stuff. (Thrusting his pelvis in an obscene macho fashion.) Power, man! Power!" (101).

Bunny is a Sardar who has cut his hair to hide his outer religious identity and has married to hide his inner gay identity. He is a success in the TV program 'Yeh Hai Hamara Parivaar'. The title of the program and its success suggest that India is a traditional society with a conventional social setup. He portrays the ideal middle class Indian, whom everyone looks up to: the 'ideal husband and father'.

Ed is also trying to 'camouflage' in the same manner as Bunny Singh. He is under immense psychological pressure and is on the verge of a nervous breakdown. On one hand he is in conflict with Kamlesh whom he leaves because he is ashamed of his relationship with him and because he does not want to be branded as a gay and thereby a misfit in the society. On the other hand, he is in conflict with Kiran, from whom he hides his true identity and tries to use her to remain in touch with Kamlesh. Sharad is the antithesis of Ed. He is comfortable with his sexuality and is vocal of his gay identity: "Let the world know that you exist. Honey if you flaunt it, you've got it" (70). He openly admits that "I am not bisexual. I am gay as a goose" (100).

In case of Bunny, homosexuality exists alongside heterosexuality. What one forgets is that when one hides the true self, acts like heterosexual and gets married, it results in many problems. The homosexual man does not love his wife, because he loves a friend of his own sex. Both Ed and Bunny are branded as 'hypocrites' cheating another woman's feelings. When Ed decides to marry Kiran, to secretly get Kamlesh's love, he forgets the emotional harm he would be doing to Kiran. Kiran asks him, "What did you want from me? What did you want from me so badly that you could not care how much you hurt me for it?" (107). Bunny and Ed thus translate the oppression they receive at the hands of society into deception and victimization of their wives: the chain reaction begins, without any point in sight at which it would end.

Dattani cleverly juxtaposes two contrasting scenarios where there is the gathering of gays in a flat on one hand, where all the action takes place and of a wedding going on offstage and sounds of celebration are quite loud and clear. The wedding is the sanctification and endorsement of a heterosexual relationship and "the whole world acknowledges two people who enter a union pact, so they have to stick by that" (72). The society approves of a heterosexual relationship but the homosexual relations are looked down upon by the majority. The gays present in the party feel the pressure of the social customs and traditions. They try to gain space and come to terms with their own identity in contrast to the social norms. Kiran, says, "I really wish they would allow gay people to marry" (98). And she gets a reply from Ranjit who says, "They do. Only not to the same sex" (98).

Ed tries to stick to the norms of the society by pretending to be 'straight' but cannot hide his true self as he has a past, a past that haunts him. Sharad pinpoints the crisis in Ed's mind through the gay anthem that he sings in the beginning and the end of the play which is the English version of Charles Aznavour's 'Comme ils disent' 'What Makes a Man a Man':

> So many times we have to pay
> For having fun and being gay.... (55-56)
> I ask myself what I have got
> And what I am and what I'm not. (101)

Deepali is another character who stands out as a sensible and seasoned lesbian, at ease with her identity and relationship with Tina. She is sympathetic and concerned for Kamlesh. Her concern for his pain is reflected in her conversation with Kamlesh, "If you were a woman, we would be in love.... If you were heterosexual, we would be married" (65). She is vocal of her sexual inclinations in her arguments at the party and says, "It's not shame, is it? With us?... Of the corners we will be pushed into where we don't want to be" (89) and of the gay cause, "I am all for the gay men's cause. Men deserve only men!" (60).

Dattani uses the symbol of the photograph to highlight the identity crisis in the play. It is a photograph where Kamlesh and Ed are hugging each other 'cheek to cheek, pelvis to pelvis, Naked' (60). It is the only photograph in Kamlesh's possession, as he has returned all the other photographs to Ed along with the negatives. He was hiding this one in the bathroom, behind the mirror which Sharad discovers and takes out to show it to all. Kamlesh finds it beautiful but Ed calls it ugly and a piece of filth. Ed's calling it ugly shows that he was not ready to leave any proof of his gay identity with Kamlesh. Overwhelmed by the circumstances and social pressures, Ed tries to commit suicide in the play. His attempt at suicide shows that he is weak and unable to sustain the identity crisis. The other characters in the play also suffer from the dichotomy of life, but they have some faith and belief in their identity and they are articulate about it in their 'bubble'. Ed does not want to reveal his true identity even to his close friends and to his girlfriend. He breaks down towards the end when his gay identity comes out in the open through his photograph with Kamlesh where both are hugging each other naked. He is in a dilemma: "Where do I begin? How do I begin to live?" (111).

Kiran is initially dumbfound at seeing the picture but then replaces the picture of her and Ed in the frame with the picture of Ed and Kamlesh, symbolizing that she considers an open gay relationship a better choice than a hidden one.

The entire experience of crisis, predicament and dilemma that the homosexuals in the play undergo, regarding their identity can be summed up in the speech of Bunny Singh in the third Act when he makes his confession in front of his gay friends and especially to Kiran when he says:

> I have denied a lot of things...you all hate me for being such a hypocrite. The people who know me are the people who hate me. That is not such a nice feeling. I have tried to survive. In both the worlds. And it seems I

> do not exist in either. I am sorry, Kiran, I lied to you as I have lied to the rest of the world. I said to you that I am a liberal-minded person. I am not them but I accept them. Actually, it is they who are liberal-minded. They have accepted me in spite of my letting them down so badly. I deny them in public, but I want their love in private. I have never told anyone in so many words what I am telling you now—I am a gay man. Everyone believes me to be the model middle-class Indian man. I was chosen for the part in the serial because I fit into common perceptions of what a family man ought to look like. I believed in it myself. I lied—to myself first. And I continue to lie to millions of people every week on Thursday nights. (102-03)

It is not just the denial of the true identity by Bunny Singh but the speech encompasses the entire gay community that is under tremendous pressure as to hide their true identity and be a charlatan so that the people of the 'acceptable world' would not hate them. All of them try to 'survive in both the worlds'. But they end up with a sense of belongingness to none. John McRae puts it as:

> ...the fault is just not the characters'—it is everyone's, in a society which not only condones but encourages hypocrisy, which demands deceit and negation, rather than allowing self-expression, responsibility and dignity. (John 45)

This experience of contradiction between the self and the society leads to the identity crisis which has been beautifully dramatized in this play. The play is a vindication of the rights of the gays who need at least some social space to overcome their identity crisis. The play ends with 'Fade out last on the picture of Ed and Kamlesh, Kiran and Kamlesh holding each other' implying the acceptance of gay identity by at least one heterosexual and revelation to the rest of the society. The picture iterates that the reality will always exist howsoever or whosoever tries to deny it.

Language in the plays of Dattani has the congruity of convincing and coherence, fitting the characters according to their social status; it is the natural outcome of tongue; only accents make the difference. It is through the use of language that play becomes more realistic. Dattani makes use of bold words in the dialogues of this play; words that a conservative Indian society does not relish publically. One doesn't have to look for gay connotations between the lines. Words like: bulge in the pants, coconut friend, buggery, dickhead, love bites, pelvis to pelvis, nerds, fucking hot, faggot, pansy, gandu etc. have been used without any restriction. These words have been taken from the gay vocabulary and used here to make the dialogues crisp and functional. Dattani makes the characters speak loud and long of their sexual desires and experiences in the play. There are quick exchanges between the characters and sometimes long monologues are used wherever and whenever necessary. Dattani realizes the needs of the theatre and he fulfils those needs in his own bold style.

> Dattani is intrinsically a theatre person, rather than a writer, is evident in the way he is able to structure the stage mechanism effectively and how at times allows the text to speak for themselves and to look at their own workings and methodology. He employs a language that is often pungent, clear and sharp, pushing the spoken word to its limits and interfering them with pregnant silence and that only someone with an intimate inwardness with theatre can. (Chaudhuri 105)

In the play, Dattani has made use of multi-level stage to represent the different spaces of household representing the mental spaces of the characters and the different realities they live in. The dark expensive area represents the mental anguish and dilemma of the characters while the open space represents the action in the context of external thoughts. All the action takes place in Kamlesh's flat that is divided into three spaces—the living room, the bedroom and the non-realistic expensive state. The flat is situated at the Marine Drive which gives the idea of the luxurious life of Mumbai. There is a contrast between the glorious view of the 'Queen's Necklace' and the isolated flat of Kamlesh which shows the contrast between the public and private life of the gays. The second is the bedroom of Kamlesh, which is hidden behind the wall which gives it an image of mystery and privacy. The third area is the space where the characters immediately suspend and their innermost thoughts and feelings come out. Chaudhuri comments in Contemporary Writers in English,

> Dattani obviously seems to have a point to make to his audience. But rather than directly preach, the playwright dramatizes and peoples the performance stage with characters one begins to identify with, facing genuine, real life problems. The play, then, in a sense, is a plea for empathy and sensitivity to India's 'queer culture'. (Chaudhuri 51)

It is clear that Dattani feels the need to establish a firm connection between the possibilities of greater space for the gays from the affluent society. He makes a plea for the acceptance and acknowledgement of the gay and lesbian community. He problematizes the whole issue of gay relationship and analyses the world of gay people expecting public participation on the problem under discussion. Dattani takes a plunge into the inner recesses of the characters who desire to be gay. It appears that they are puzzled about their identity in society and they feel marginalized. If they fulfil their longing to be gay individuals, it will damage their identities and recognition in society which disapproves such a relationship and promotes marriage between heterosexuals. Their sexuality is endangered and engulfed by the rules and regulations of the society.

Torn between longing and identity, the characters try to find out their alternatives. The clash results from their conflicting nature with the culture of the society to which they belong. As Bijay Kumar Das comments in *Form and Meaning in Mahesh Dattani's Plays*:

> There is a binary opposition between their nature and the culture of their society. This dichotomy between nature and culture obstructs their love and poisons their minds. The note of revolt against the society is unmistakable. In the page of globalization, nature triumphs over culture. (Das 97-98)

Dattani discusses the homosexuality as it features in our society. He shows how established norms of society suppress and repress individual urge and passion causing mental agony to the person. He neither approves nor disapproves the marriage between the people of the same sex. He just unmasks the truth shrouded under established tradition of heterosexual relationship. Dattani's theatrical creed asserts that human nature has its own autonomous space. Any act of encroachment on this space, either through conventional ideology or by any other means, will result into agitation and uprising causing chaos and destruction.

Works Cited

Chaudhuri, Asha Kuthari. *Contemporary Writers in English Mahesh Dattani.* New Delhi: Foundation Books Pvt Ltd., 2005. Print.

Das, Bijay Kumar. *Form and Meaning in Mahesh Dattani's Plays.* New Delhi: Atlantic Publishers & Distributors (P) Ltd., 2008. Print.

Dattani, Mahesh. *Collected Plays.* New Delhi: Penguin Books. 2000. Print. (The figures in the brackets pertaining to *On a Muggy Night in Mumbai* are from this source.)

McRae, John. "A Note on the Play." *Collected Plays by Mahesh Dattani.* New Delhi: Penguin Books, 2000. Print.

8

Unravelling the Matrix of *Seven Steps Around the Fire*

Deepa Vanjani

Mahesh Dattani's dramatic world is inhabited by characters marginalized by society due to their sexual preferences—gays, lesbians, transsexuals, by thwarted dreams, hopes, by the predicaments of modern society. His is a sordid world of grim realities. The idea is to focus the lens of his eye on all that's around, visible or invisible, and to bring to the surface issues, less discussed or highlighted in the literary world, but not necessarily to seek a solution.

Dattani is known for the bold themes he takes up in his plays and their treatment. It is said he talks of invisible issues as gay and lesbian relationships, incest and transgenders, post-modernist issues to say. But it is not that the issues are invisible, they are unutterable. *Brief Candle, Dance Like a Man, Mango Souffle (*a screenplay*), On a Muggy Night in Mumbai, Tara, Thirty Days in September* and the film script *Ek Alag Mausam* (that grapples with the theme of AIDS) are plays that deal with such issues.

Like Vijay Tendulkar, Dattani's plays too are set against the backdrop of a hostile society. He presents modern day man and his life in all its crudity and complexity. There is no desire to moralize or philosophize. He just lays bare man, his desires, his struggle against society and social norms. More often than not, Mahesh Dattani just portrays the degeneration of the social milieu and man, revealing the inherent tendencies of human nature. Again like Tendulkar, Dattani explores in his plays the alienation of the modern individual to contemporary politics, subtleties of man-woman relationship, complexities of human character and socio-psychological tensions.

In a sense, he is a playwright who has chosen to grapple with bold themes in a forthright manner. *Seven Steps Around the Fire* is one such play in the body of his work. The play, first broadcast by BBC on 9 January 1999, makes us think about the homogenizing role of society, which in turn creates a tug of war between the demands of society and its hegemony in individual life and individual identities, dreams and perceptions. It lays bare the treatment meted out to eunuchs/transgenders by society for they do not fit into the pattern of the gendered identity which stereotypes people. The transgender issue has existed in India since the days of *Mahabharata* where in Shikhandi played a pivotal role in the killing of Bhisham. There are subtle references to the lack of financial empowerment of women in India.

The plot of the play revolves around the murder of Kamla, a eunuch, whose sister Anarkali has been falsely implicated for the crime and is imprisoned. The protagonist Uma, a lecturer of Sociology, wife of Suresh, superintendent of police, gets involved in the lives of the *hijras* while working on her thesis. When she meets Anarkali in jail, in presence of constable Munnswamy, she is drawn into the vortex of their secrets and their lives. She is led to Champa, the woman who is the head of the *hijras*, and through her subsequently unravels the innocence of Anarkali. She learns of the affair of Kamla, the most beautiful among the eunuchs, with the minister's son Subbu. The two get married secretly. A photograph of the two, taken on their wedding day, opens the pandora's box. Kamla is disposed off by the minister's order. Subbu's marriage is fixed with a respectable girl. On the wedding day, however, when Subbu sees Champa and Anarkali dancing at the venue of his marriage, he shoots himself. The matter is hushed up. The incident is proven to be an accident. The truth of Kamla's death is never revealed. The reasons being the power muscles flexed by the minister. In doing so Dattani also holds for our study the police-politics nexus which in itself raises many questions about our democratic set-up and the condition of human rights in our society.

Tendulkar in his play 'Dambadwipcha Mukabala' [Encounter in Umbugland] too "unveils the essential nature of the game of politics", as Arundhati Banerjee mentions in her introduction to the book *Vijay Tendulkar: Five Plays*. Interestingly Tendulkar in the same play uses a eunuch named Prannarayan as the sutradhar or narrator and through this character he unfolds the central focus of the play—the futility of power. *Seven Steps Around the Fire*, though not a play given entirely to the expose of political intrigues, also brings this sub-theme to the surface. The thrust of the play by Dattani is not limited to politics alone. It is also a question mark on society's acceptance of certain sections and the rawness that surrounds us and how love is often nipped in the bud due to societal norms. He punctuates the play with Uma's interior monologues using them as a technique to voice the playwright's concerns and views.

To make the inner thought in the mind of his characters, he introduced the technique of 'thought' instead of 'asides' in his plays. Thought is followed by speech in commensurate with the themes of the play. There is a lot of code mixing (i.e. Indian words, Hindi words, for example written in English) in his plays (Das 124).

Uma voices the thoughts which in essence constitute the crux of the play. Paradoxically Uma, a Sociology lecturer, daughter of the Vice-Chancellor, is educated and financially independent. Yet she doesn't have enough money at her disposal and is answerable to her husband Suresh for the money she spends. She is permitted to do her research, but is to be escorted by constable Munnswamy under all conditions. The sexual relationship with Suresh is demanding, as is revealed by the brief intimate encounter between husband and wife described in the play, at a point where Uma is mentally preoccupied, while Suresh is interested in sex. The patriarchal mindset is revealed through Suresh's words, "Look, it is one thing that I am allowing you to go through these cases for your thesis, but don't feel any compassion for them.... Keep your soft heart for me" (42).

There is a great deal of discussion on the issues of human rights and their violation around us. But whom does society regard as human? Are those, who are on the periphery, not fit to be treated as humans? These are questions which came to my mind when I read the play. Kamla, Champa, Anarkali, the transgenders in the play being discussed, are more marginalized than the marginalized because they are neither male nor female. According to our norms, the male represents power, force, and domination while the female represents the creator. Biologically one is a man or a woman by virtue of one's anatomy. Kamla and others do not belong to any category. They are the cursed ones deprived of marriage, family, offspring and therefore they do not fit into the mould cast by society. They are the 'others', robbed of human value and meaning. Gender relationships, and the plight of eunuchs, who are neither male nor female, but wanting to be either, are depicted in his play artistically as well as realistically.

In creating an identity the otherness syndrome plays a major role. The 'gaze' is in itself sufficient to decide, to judge and to typecast one's identity and this gaze creates 'otherness'. In J.M. Coetzee's novel *Disgrace* the role of gaze is aptly drawn out in the scene where David Lurie and his daughter Lucy, when attending Petrus' party, are stared at, for they are the only whites present in the party, in the black-dominated South Africa.

Identity is pluralistic since we have many identities wrapped into one, though a particular identity may be hegemonic either in a particular situation or most of the times. We associate it with sex, gender, religion, geographical region, race and many other things. And we are not, most of us, transcendentalists who explain matter and objective things as products of the subjective mind. We judge identity by identity markers. "The salience of identity for Indians is evident in the plethora of marks of identification in their socio-cultural landscape...Indians carry multiple identities... depending on the context in which an individual is behaving, he or she will selectively invoke a given identity" (Jayaram 129).

Gender/sex orientation and sexual preferences also become reasons for otherness. What do these terms signify? Sex refers to biological differences between males and females. Gender refers to the meanings that we decipher of these biological differences and the individual and social aspects of masculinity and feminity. Since it is with our bodies that we act, and since psychological and social factors can affect our bodies, there is a great deal of debate about the relationship between sex and gender.

Gays, lesbians, transgenders and transsexuals are not a part of the social mainstream; the acceptance level for them is minimal in a country like India. The issue of their rights has gained some momentum in recent years with some activists leading the scene, but we still have a long way to go. In the words of Iris Young "The very act of defining a gender excludes or devalues some bodies, practices and discourses at the same time that it obscures the constructed, and thus, contestable character of that gender identity.... Gender discourse tends to reify the fluid and shifting social processes in which people relate, communicate, play, work, struggle with one another..." (qtd. in Irene Gedalof 176).

If feminism describes women as powerless victims of patriarchy, how do we define the others such as eunuchs or transsexuals?

Transgenders and eunuchs are confronted with a conflict between their anatomical make up and the emotional and psychological one. A man may feel like a woman and vice versa. While for eunuchs life is deprived of human dignity. They live by singing and dancing at births, on festivals and in marriages. Paradoxically both fertility rituals—birth and marriage—are denied to them. "The two events in mainstream Hindu culture where their presence is acceptable—marriage and birth—ironically are the very same privileges denied to them by man and nature" (Dattani 10-11).

Uma dwells on the nature of the eunuch community; about where they come from and why do they have an obsession with birth and weddings. She wonders if what her mother said about them putting a curse on people if displeased proved true for them. Did they put a curse on their family when they were not allowed to sing and dance at their wedding? When she attempts to unfold the mystery surrounding Kamla's death, Champa warns her and tells her, "Go home to your husband" (35). The words husband and home are significant and have an underlying element of pathos for while Uma has this security, Champa, Anarkali and the likes have none. It is paradoxical that *hijras* in the play know and speak the truth, while the men who know the truth but don't speak it, are men of position. The play ends with Uma's agonizing observation, "They know, Anarkali, Champa and all the *hijra* people knew who was behind the killing of Kamla. They have no voice" (42).

Kamla, the beautiful eunuch, the unravelling of whose murder mystery, leads to the action of the play, stands out for she envisions for herself a happily married life like any other woman. This stepping out proves to be disastrous for her and Subbu. In love with Subbu, the minister's son, Kamla marries him. For one who is already cursed, this proves to be a double jinx. How could a high profile minister accept a eunuch as his daughter-in-law? So Kamla must be extricated. The murder is carried out. The police know the truth. But the Minister cannot be touched. Instead Anarkali is accused and arrested. Dattani brings to light the fact that society creates ghettos where people not belonging to the mainstream mould are thrown into, be it due to gender or religion or caste.

It is a vicious circle of slavery, though of a different kind, into which the modern man is trapped. In an article published in *New York Times* and that was carried in *Hindustan Times* on 7 November 2013, Nicholas D. Kristof writes of 21st century slavery against the backdrop of the movie *12 Years a Slave*. He cites that according to the Global Slavery Index released recently, the US is home to about 60,000 people who can be called modern versions of slaves. These are not slaves sold in auctions, but "include illegal immigrants forced to work without pay under threat of violence and teenage girls coerced to sell sex and hand all the money to their pimps". The relevance of this reference here is to bring to mind how society perpetuates violence on sections of the population in different ways and the need to shake ourselves out of cozy definitions of normalcy and acceptance. This also is a pointer at how power operates by repositioning and by exclusion.

John McRae made the following observation about the play *On a Muggy Night in Mumbai* also by Mahesh Dattani, "It is a play about how society creates patterns of behaviour and how easy it is for individuals to fall victim to the expectations society creates" (45). The same can be true of *Seven Steps Around the Fire*.

Also our norms of love and sex are stereotyped. They are not just aspects of the body. Society imposes restrictions on individuals. So the relationship between Kamla and Subbu also cannot be accepted.

Anarkali is subjected to sexual abuse in police custody. For constable Munnswamy, Anarkali is 'chi' and 'it'. Uma addresses Anarkali as 'her', giving a human tag to her dehumanized existence. Anarkali cannot hope for justice. She can't speak the truth, though she knows it. But she leads Uma to Champa and thus leads her to unravel the truth. I wish to focus on the marginalization on the basis of gender and identity crisis for Dattani's sensitivity towards this comes forth as one delves into the play and discerns this undercurrent. He plunges into the heart of the characters engrossed in reality and plagued by societal discrimination.

We also grapple with the question of love that can't be unhinged from sexual connotations in social terms, thus nibbling the possibility of platonic love. It is the beauty and not the gender which lures the minister's son Subbu in the play to marry the *hijra* Kamla, implying that she can be extremely charming though biologically dysfunctional, which should be kept in abeyance. Why insist for the physical when the relationship can be Platonic? The aesthetics can transcend into indescribable ecstasy. John Donne, in his poem *The Extasie*, clearly specifies that it is not sex, it is just the touch or riveted eyes which transports one to ecstasy.

Donne speaks of transcendental love, love that is beyond the physical, which transports the lovers into realms of ecstasy. When they are together they achieve the state of this lofty platonic pleasure just by gazing into each other's eyes, just by looking at each other, just by being in each other's presence. It is a culmination and consummation on the sentient plane, not sexual. It then becomes love sublime—a supreme bliss. Just by the sight or touch or fragrance of the beloved, one enters into the world of disembodied pleasure which is beyond the physical.

The beauty of the lover is a catalyst transporting the beholder into this 'extasie'. Even though both are present at the moment, yet they are not, they are lost. Yet this is not an annihilation of identity. In it one views the divine.

> This extasie doth unperplex
>
> (We said) and tell us what we love,
>
> Wee see by this, it was not sexe,
>
> Wee see, we saw not what did move.... (qtd. in Herbert J.C. Grierson, 16-17)

The love of Kamla and Subbu is such. It is beyond the limitations of sex and gender. Their marriage is unique for though it cannot be consummated through a sexual relationship, both Kamla and Subbu are so much in love that this aspect doesn't stand in the way of their getting married. Such is the beauty of Kamla, that nothing else matters for Subbu. Though dysfunctional sexually, the relationship is complete in itself. Subbu is mystified by the beauty of his beloved. It elates him, transposing him into the state of ecstasy that Donne points at, "when love, with one another so/ interanimates two soules...".

In a way Dattani has brought to the forefront an hitherto undealt with aspect of a man-woman relationship in his play *Seven Steps Around the Fire*. He talks of love that goes beyond societal norms of sex and gender. The essence of their love lies therein. For the world, however, it is unacceptable. The piety of the relationship lies waste for it does not fall into the bracket of normalcy, thus resulting in the tragic death of Kamla and Subbu. In a way it questions our norms of love, sex and relationships. A man [Subbu] cannot love a *hijra*. A *hijra's* place is not in the world of 'straight' men and women. Such is the intensity of the love that Subbu kills himself in the anguish of losing his beloved.

Writes Erin Mee, "His characters struggle for some kind of freedom and happiness under the weight of tradition, cultural constructions of gender, and repressed desire.... In his plays Dattani takes on what he called the 'invisible issues' of Indian society" (320).

"Engrossed in contemporary reality, his characters seek remedy of their ills and sufferings caused by poverty and societal discrimination" (Das 24). Such are the characters who fill the canvas of the play *Seven Steps Around the Fire*. Through their struggles and their fate we discern the established patterns of our society and scratch under the surface to view its harsh undulating face in the eye.

Works Cited

Banerjee, Arundhati. Introduction, *Vijay Tendulkar: Five Plays*. New Delhi: OUP, 1996. Print.

Das, Bijay Kumar. *Form and Meaning in Mahesh Dattani's Plays*. New Delhi: Atlantic Publishers and Distributors, 2008. Print.

Dattani, Mahesh. *Seven Steps Around the Fire*. Meerut: Sahil Print Media, 2013. Print.

Gedalof, Irene. "Power, Identity and Impure Spaces." *Rethinking Identity with Indian and Western Feminisms*. New York: Routledge, 1999. Print.

Jayaram, N. "Identity: A Semantic Exploration in India's Society and Culture." *Keywords: Identity*, ed. Nadia Tazc. New Delhi: Vistaar Publications, 2004. Print.

Kristof, Nicholas D. *Hindustan Times*. "Still in Shackles of a Different Kind": November 7, 2013. Print.

McRae, John. "A Note on the Play." *On a Muggy Night in Mumbai. Collected Plays*. New Delhi: Penguin Books, 2000. Print.

Mee, Erin. "A Note on the Play." *Tara. Collected Plays*. New Delhi: Penguin Books, 2006. Print.

9

A Conversation on Gender Rights, IPC 377 and Its Aftermath with Reference to *Do the Needful*

Gunasekharan Dharmaraja

Background

There died Indian culture and gave rise to western imported culture. If hostels suffer from water scarcity problem, if teachers are not satisfied with their students' results, if an engineering student gets caught mobile-handedly in her hostel, all are due to the removal of 377 and its aftermath. None of them in India who give importance to so-called culture could digest Delhi High Court's mud-slinging verdict on Indian's so-called cultural face. Everything is doomed and there would be no rain in India from now on. The Kalyuga has ripened. Indian Penal Code 377 is repealed.

On the other side, celebrations are carried out in the streets of this semi-feudal and semi-colonial India. The standard ring tones of cell phone SMS rang out India's arrival into the arena of respecting fundamental rights. These are the two views one could see in India after the judgment was passed by the Delhi High court on July 2, 2009 on IPC 377, the draconian Indian Penal Code that penalized the same sex activity and the so-called unnatural sexes.

Introduction

As the origin of transgenders, there are two types of arguments on the origin of same sexes. One is "LGBTs are born".

Scientists believe that increase or decrease of chromosomes is the only reason for the birth of LGBT (Lesbian, Gays, Bisexuals, Transgender). There are only twenty-three pairs of chromosomes in a human cell. Every human being has twenty-three pairs of chromosomes. Among the twenty-three pairs of chromosomes, the twenty-third pair of chromosome will decide a baby male or female. X chromosome that can produce feminine gender joins with Y chromosome that can produce masculine gender. If X of male and X of female join, the born baby is female. If Y of male and X of female join, the baby is male. Thus, one can have the understanding that XY is male and XX is female. Sometimes if one more X or Y chromosome adds itself with the "supposed to be united chromosomes" neither male nor female gender will be born. When the neuter gender baby is born, it does not have any identity of a transgender. But when it grows up, its identities slowly changes; they dedicate themselves to be complete transgenders. At the same time, this rule cannot be applicable to the origin of LGBTs in a natural and strict manner.

The second opinion is that LGBTs are not born; but made. Anthropologists totally differ from scientists' above said point of view. They feel transgenders are evolved due to the brought up and social activities. All the characters of masculine and feminine genders are socialized. A baby is born without any manly or womanly behaviour. Only when it grows up, does it inculcate the behaviour and character of a man or a woman according to its environment.

LGBTs are not responsible for the above said problems. If one believes in God, God should be blamed for the birth of the innocent and cursed transgenders. Otherwise the responsibility shall be shifted to the scientists who are supposed to find out the 'abnormal chromosomes' from the human cells of new born babies to avoid the birth of these unfortunate people as Su. Samuthiram requested in his preface to his book *Transgender*. If circumstances and situations are responsible for their different kinds of brought ups, those circumstances should be eliminated.

The sexual orientations of these people totally confuse the people who do not have a broad and open-minded approach towards the genders and their sexual orientations. Even one's patriarchal approaches on sexual orientations lead him/her to disrespect the LGBTs. Anyways, in the aspect of intelligence and heritability; studies have shown that genetic factors in the birth are the deciding factors than the environmental factors for the birth of innocent LGBTs. Thus one could understand the fact that LGBTs are not the byproducts of western imported culture and just a decade problem, but they have been here as everybody else does and they have their own hidden history.

Indian Penal Code was drafted by Lord McCauley and introduced in 1861 in British India. Section 377 IPC is contained in chapter XVI of the IPC titled "Of offences affecting the Human body (From Delhi High Court's Judgment on 377). This British drafted Indian Penal Code criminalizes the carnal intercourse and other unnatural sexual activities. The repealed IPC does not trespass the privacy of LGBTs alone, but also has its octopus hands trespassing into the bedrooms of heterosexuals.

Moreover, LGBTs are accused of spreading AIDS. Most of those who oppose these repealing 377 cry out loudly about the sexually transmitted diseases. They merely keep saying that allowing or permitting LGBTs to execute their sexual orientations would lead to the immediate spread of AIDS, as if LGBTs are the only means of STDs or, as if all LGBTs have taken an oath to spread deadly HIV+ and AIDS to everyone. The concern here if the point of talk is about the spreading of HIV+, surely it should be taken into account seriously. But if people go by the arguments of these recent day health care takers that LGBT sexual orientation is the reason for spreading of HIV+, we have to get rid of these LGBT sexual orientations. But at the same time, as far as medical reports are concerned, the unsafe heterosexual sexual mode is the main reason for the spread of HIV+. So in order to avoid sexually transmitted diseases, we can criminalize all the sexual activities including LGBTs and including the majority heterosexual activities.

Those who strive hard for the fundamental rights of human society too oppose LGBTs. They believe that sex should be for reproduction alone. Without the point of reproduction in its core, all other sexes and sexual activities will be considered as the Western import by the right fundamentalist; bourgeoisies' destructive culture by the leftists. The reason behind this takes people to the hunter-gatherer society. Hunter-gatherer society relies on the manual power of human beings where the matriarchal system was banned and the leading role of women was confiscated. "The overthrow of mother right was the world historical defeat of the female sex" says Engels. More number of human beings can hunt more number of animals or they can produce more food that could solve the needs of human beings in times of scarcity. So men and women were in a position to beget more number of children. Thus sex was restricted for begetting children who in turn would bring more food to the community. To gain more production, hunter-gatherer society implemented strict sexual rules on the females to produce more off-springs. Though the age of hunter-gather dusks, the hangover of the age and the remnants of feudalism (blood relations are only relations well constructed by casteism in Indian society) are not ready to recognize other sexual activities in which no child can be produced, especially in the sexual activities of LGBTs. In the name of majority and age-old customs and traditions, a single soul's right cannot be denied. But today, India does not allow a human being's basic right to decide himself/herself to live as per his/her sexual orientation. When the basic idea for sexual activities in the hunter-gatherer society was for more production, the super-structure of the hunter-gatherer society was also framed in such a way that those activities that are not for the off-spring production are anti-religious. So all religions, the main propaganda agency of superstructure of the state, without any exception ban LGBTs and have considered and declared LGBTs sexual orientations as anti-religious. For example, Hindu Dharma considers abortion as a major sin. But Islam practices it. Roman Catholics too ban abortion and if all these religions believe that even abortion is anti-religious, there will be no question to discuss the rights of LGBTs. Religious fanatics and the propaganda agencies of male dominated hunter-gatherer society are on the way against Delhi court's judgment. The views of the leftists are very much a shock to the LGBT supporters. Though the parliamentary left parties in their press statement support Delhi High court's judgment, they do not wholeheartedly support the LGBT issue. Surely their true colors will be exposed if there be one homosexual in their party, as we have a good example right in front, who are none but Nepal Maoist who theoretically want the discussion about LGBTs, but they fight the LGBTs in the streets. The reason for this understanding is very simple. These half baked intellectuals have the understanding that sex is for reproduction alone (but with a wholehearted permission from women) any sexual activity apart from this reason can and will be considered as lust and bourgeoisie culture. For these like-minded people we have a question to ask. If intercourse is for reproduction alone, why do couples remain united even after they beget children? Can we make a law to separate the couples those who remain together after the birth of enough number of children? At last all these questions can be boiled down to a single understanding that is sex is either for reproduction or for pleasure. All intellectuals even those who support LGBTs are afraid of this single statement—sex for pleasure, as it would tarnish the ideal family system of India and other countries. The one man who was not carried away by all these family sentiments was Periyar E.V. Ramasamy. He was the one who opposed women begetting children. He sternly believed that begetting children make women inferior, weak and a slave of family sentiments. But unfortunately, we do not have that legendary man now to support LGBTs, 'the sex doers of pleasure'.

Bureaucrats are on the way to protect Indian culture as they believe that LGBTs are viruses let loose by the Delhi High court by its recent judgment. We could come across from some of our students about these precautions to protect the dilapidated Indian families. In women's colleges, any notable intimacy between two girls is sternly warned. In hostel rooms girls are warned not to stay in pairs as they may indulge in lesbian activities. As a notable Homo activist Gaudam Bhan participated in an NDTV program, the Superintendent of Police of Mangalore city worried that repealing of 377 would give conduciveness for the hostel students to indulge in illegal sex. But the above said bureaucrats and state machineries forget or pretend to ignore that Articles 21, 14 and 15 of Indian Constitution that supports the fundamental rights of human beings and which give equality of opportunity and equality before law to every citizen, irrespective of caste, creed, place or sex. And it gives freedom to those who are above 18 years to have sex with anybody with a mutual consent if they desire. The above 18 years college student citizens cannot be an exception to this.

When I had a chat with Sunil, an FTM, Sunil argued not to address their sexual orientation as unnatural. Unnatural would mean that LGBTs do it deliberately; but the practice is not so. So we could change that word as common/uncommon or famous/infamous or majority/minority instead of natural/unnatural. Similarly people question when they are introduced to Homosexuals as to whether they are homos. To this, Dattani's reply was quite interesting. He commented that if LGBTs are questioned, "Are you a homo?" to be introduced, then the heterosexuals also have to be questioned, "Are you a heterosexual?"

This Indian society that still has remnants of feudalism in its core has made some so-called values and yard sticks to scale it in the name of culture to survive at the declining stage of it. The horrible face of this feudal society can easily be identified when it never recognizes the personal interest and desires (it does not affect the so-called nation's interest) of the people. It starts from individual's freedom to a group of people's. Karan Thappar, a notable journalist answered the question of Arun Jetley in *Devil's Advocate* in the New Year special interview in CNN-IBN about the separatists of Kashmir, by asking, "when one does not like to be an Indian, why should we pull him to be united?" The verse of a Telugu poem goes—"Dhesam Annthi Mannukathu Manusalu" (nation is not land; but people). So likes and dislikes of common people are equally important as the likes and dislikes of state or the majority. In the name of majority and age-old customs and traditions, a single soul's right cannot be denied. But today, India does not allow a human being's basic right to decide himself to live as a male or a female though he or she is born with male or female organs. If you are born with male organs, however much your mind cries, the society never allows you to change as you desire to live. If you are born as a male and though you feel as a woman, you have no other option than to live like a man withstanding to all criticisms and obscene comments of the male dominated society, but cannot convert yourself to the other being. Even inside one's bedroom, the state peeps through the window and restricts people from having 'state-called' or the 'so-called' unnatural sexes. It advises couples to have only the male dominated sex. If one goes for innovative methods, he/she may be punished for doing so. If this is the condition for the married male-female couples then the condition of the Subaltern people like Homos and Lesbians are worse. Indians speak as if no Indian has extra-marital sex, nobody is a homo, and particularly none among their women is a Lesbian. But almost every year the red-handedly caught girls from women's hostels have torn up the curtain truth to lime light. The society has made its own values and customs and it asks people to follow it or at least to live up to its expectations in daylight. But behind the curtain, one is free to do anything. If one wishes to marry a girl belonging to a lower caste, the society will oppose him. But if he just goes for illegal sex with her, this society would accompany him. Faithfully, the state will let it go and keep its eyes blind-folded. So if you are a freedom fighter, you have to be against the so-called values and customs. Only by the name of these values and customs people of this nation are suppressed. So is the story with Mahesh Dattani's play *Do the Needful*. The main characters of this play maintain 'Teri bhi chup, Meri bhi chup', since the society allows them to be secretive in doing what it opposes.

Before sinking into discussion, here is the outline of the play *Do the Needful* in short. Alpesh Patel is the son of Chandrakant Patel and Kusumben Patel. Lata Gowda is the daughter of Devraj Gowda and Prema Gowda. Alpesh Patel is a homo whereas Lata is straight. Alpesh does not want to marry a girl since his first marriage with a girl was a broken one since he is a homo. Lata is in love with a guy named Salim who is in Mumbai. Alpesh never wants to share his life with a girl. Simultaneously Lata does not wish to marry anyone other than Salim. But both are compelled (by their parents) to fulfill their parents' wish by their marriage. Though both the bride's and the groom's parents have their own caste dignity they could not uphold it in their children's marriage as their children's 'immorality' is well known (known to their own caste people; if is not known to their own caste people, then it is not immoral at all).

Alpesh is a homosexual but for a time being he is forced (by none other than his own parents) to be a bi-sexual. But after his first marriage fails (heterosexual marriage I mean) he wishes to lead his life as a homo. Let us take a closer look at his life.

In the beginning Alpesh tells us who he is. "Is Trilok free?... He knows exactly where my tight spots are..." (119).

Though the above given words look like those that can be normally spoken by even straight people, after knowing Alpesh we understand why he has spoken so. He knows very well that living with a woman is impossible for him.

> Alpesh. Baa, I want to ask you something.
>
> Kusumben Patel. Yes?
>
> Alpesh. Is it...is it very important for me to get married?
>
> Pause
>
> Kusumben Patel. Hmm.
>
> Alpesh (Thought). Trilok, you can't say I didn't try.
>
> Kusumben Patel. Why do you ask me that?
>
> Alpesh. What if.... I don't want to get married.
>
> Kusumben Patel. Why don't you want to get married?
>
> Alpesh. Because I am happy being alone.
>
> ....
>
> ....
>
> Alpesh. What happened with my last marriage...
>
> Kusumben Patel. Yes? What do you want to say?
>
> Alpesh. You don't want it to happen again, do you?
>
> Pause
>
> Kusumben Patel. Are you threatening me that it will happen again?
>
> Alpesh. I am suggesting that you should be prepared for that. (Pause) She wanted the separation. It was not in my control!

> Kusumben Patel. Oh I see. And you feel...it might happen again?
>
> Alpesh. It might.
>
> Kusumben Patel. Tell me why you feel it might happen again.
>
> Alpesh. (Thought) I was not going to say it. She wanted me to.
>
> Pause
>
> Kusumben Patel. No. I will not let it happen again, it can never happen again. I might as well take poison and die if it happens again. (125-26)

Alpesh who is a homo knows very well that he cannot lead a sexually peaceful life with a girl. So in a hidden tone he tells this to his mother Kusumben Patel. There exists a situation in his home where he could not speak out loud and open what he feels or what he wishes to do with himself in life. Even when his mother asks him to pick up Swamiji from the Airport, he merely whispers a no but is forced to obey it.

> Kusumben Patel. (on the phone). Yes. yes...Hmm........ Alpesh will pick him and bring him here...
>
> Alpesh (Whispering his protest). No! (124)

So we come to the understanding that Alpesh wishes with all his heart to be a Homo but the society does not let him be one, nor allow him to claim himself as a homo. He also knows very well that his parents will never accept it as well and they might go to the extreme of committing suicide than letting him be a homosexual.

So when he wishes to meet Trilok in Slim Gym. He informs his subordinate Joseph that he was "caught in traffic Jam" and his "carburetor needs a cleanup". And he "might as well take it to the garage now...."

When he was compelled by his mother he says, "Yes. All right. I give up. If you like her, I will marry her." Threatening one tearfully will easily make him surrender and he would become a slave in front of tear bombs (*Adimai Vilanku* (Enslaved Animal) by Che. Ganesa Lingam). So he surrenders before the tear bombs of his mother and father. But he still wishes to escape from marrying a girl by reasoning out his first marriage failure to his father.

In this play, he has (mentally satisfied) sex with two guys named Trilok and Mali. It appears as if he loves Trilok but when he gets an opportunity to have sex with Mali, he does it without any hesitation.

The above-mentioned story of Alpesh is a story of every Homo in the world, or at least in India. It seems that all homos behave like those in the pre-communal society, i.e. no restriction for their sexual life (not free sex in today's context but in pre-communal society's context). But though the origin of marriage (between man and woman) is the significant process in the male dominated society for its disempowerment of women, it restricts family as one woman-one man. On account of that change free sex is felt as a sin due to the fact that marriage becomes legalized. When male-female couples are knitted together to live together legally, they will have the conducive atmosphere to lead a mentally and sexually peaceful life. Then the next code of conduct that is, having sex with someone outside marriage is illegal, becomes a widely accepted fact. Accusing homosexuals as sex mongers without making a peaceful atmosphere for them to lead a happy life, is nothing but reductionism. Forgetting the role of the society and majority mass and having an understanding that being a Homosexual is a sin and accusing that Homos are lustful is nothing but horrible reductionism. So here we cannot find fault with Homos for their activities (every one of us would have experienced a touch from a homo while traveling by bus especially).

Is Lata an Immoral Woman?

Now let us have an Umbrella view on Lata. She 'loves' a Muslim boy and she has had sex with him. Having sex with that 'terrorist' is not at all a problem to her "broadminded" parents. So her mother advises her.

> Prema Gowda. You should have thought of our lives before sleeping with that terrorist.
>
> ...You have ruined our lives!

...She has to do it in his hostel! Couldn't they go to a hill station or somewhere?

So here as far as Lata's parents are concerned, having premarital sex even with a terrorist does not matter; but it should be done behind the curtain. When Lata understands that their parents "wouldn't have allowed her to go to a hill station", she has done it in her boyfriend's hostel. But now that becomes a problem to her parents. Her mother tearfully says:

Prema Gowda. (Tearfully) All those boys knew about that. (122)

This is an example for the so-called Indian culture. Are homos there in Indian Culture? Yes. Extramarital relationship and premarital sex are also present in India. But the feudal Indian mind is never ready to accept the surviving 'bitter' truth. It turns a blind eye and ignores these existing problems. Similarly it wishes to annihilate the subalterns as if they are viruses of this country by not lending ears to their cries and pleas. When her parents come to know that Lata has an affair with a Muslim boy, and that she has had sex with him they try their best to conceal it from their caste people, and when they could not, they simply become "broad-minded" to select a bridegroom from a different caste. But they were never interested in their daughter's choice. They tearfully threaten their daughter to obey them.

Teri bhi chup, meri bhi chup (your silence and my silence)

At last the two families, Lata's and Alpesh's did the needful. Now the two characters who are suffering the marriage they dislike (being given freedom) meet as part of their parents' doing the needful.

At night when Alpesh was smoking a cigarette, he was seen by Lata. Fortunately, Lata is also a smoker. So they come to a mutual agreement that they both would not reveal their smoking to each other's parents.

Alpesh. Please don't tell my dad...about my smoking.

Lata. Its okay, I understand.

....

....

> Lata. I just came down here to join you for a smoke.
>
> Alpesh. Oh.
>
> Lata. May I have one?
>
> Alpesh. Oh, sure.
>
> Alpesh fishes out a cigarette and lights it for her. Lata exhales loud and slow.
>
> Alpesh. Teri bhi chup, meri bhi chup…'your silence and my silence'. (142)

At first they come to one common understanding that smoking is not a mistake, but their parents oppose it as a grave sin. So they do it without their knowledge and have made a mutual agreement of not revealing it.

Similar agreement and understanding continues when she knows that Alpesh is a homo. But before knowing that, she tells Alpesh very openly that she is not interested in marrying him. She plans to elope to Salim who also resides in Mumbai. Alpesh too accepts this since he is also not interested to marry a girl. But the main problem they both face is 'who would bell the cat' in the sense, as to who would reveal their mutual disinterest in their marriage to their parents. So their first meeting ends without a solution. But the entire situation changes when Alpesh gets caught by Lata who is on the way to run away from her house, while he was having sex with her servant Mali.

> Lata. You!
>
> (Thought) They were…doing it!
>
> (Speech) You are a homo. (153)
>
> When Mali begged Lata to marry Alpesh, Alpesh openly accepts his inability in making her sexually happy.
>
> I cannot make you happy. (155)

When Alpesh comes to know Lata is running away, he is very much happy.

> Alpesh. Oh, great! So you are running away! Thank you. Mali and I will help you get on a bus…. (155)

Now Lata comes to an agreement with Alpesh and their logic is too simple. Alpesh is a homo who is not interested to have sex with her. Lata is interested in Salim. But as they cannot challenge their parents' decisions, they decide to marry so that she can have her life with Salim and Alpesh can remain a homo. Initially, Alpesh is reluctant but later agrees to it on a condition that Mali should come as a dowry.

> Lata. Why should I run away! Mali has made me a sense.
>
> Alpesh. You believe what he said? What did he say anyway?
>
> Lata. What was that Hindi expression you'd used? Something about your silence and mine as well...
>
> Pause.
>
> Alpesh. No. I mean, no, I can't marry you.
>
> Lata. Are you going to say no to your parents then?
>
> Alpesh. No. (Pause.) Will you bring Mali as your dowry? (155-56)

At last they get married and they lead their lives happily. She everyday goes, lives and has sex with Salim as she wished and Alpesh also does the same.

If Alpesh was given his freedom by his parents and the state to be a homosexual, he would not have horns on his forehead and become a cuckold. But being a subaltern himself, he gives full freedom to his wife though he would become a laughing-stock.

Now what will be our understanding towards this relationship? Obscene, immoral. A lot many adjectives might also be added. But human right activists should support them. Because, if the relationship what they have is judged immoral, it is their parents are solely responsible for their immorality. The society that upholds the so-called values and principles of feudalism which never restricts their parents to offer freedom to them is also heavily chargeable and responsible. If the Society, People and the State had done the needful i.e. giving freedom to Alpesh to live as a Homosexual as per his sexual orientation, he would not have cheated his parents. If Lata's parents had allowed her to marry a "terrorist", she would not have had sex with him illegally. Their parents thought that arranging marriage for their children is needful, but their children have cheated them and they did their own needful. So the people, especially the subalterns like LGBTs are pushed to do things 'immorally' and maintain secrecy as they are not offered their freedom which they rightly deserve. Till the society is willing to engage them as human beings, the conversation is not possible. The voices unheard can make them do things secretly. The legal changes that happened in India deserve appreciation, but how those changes are incorporated in the minds of Indian people holds the card.

Works Cited

Beena, Agrawal. *Mahesh Dattani's Plays: A New Horizon in Indian Theater*. India: Book Enclave, 2008. Print.

Bible Society of World. *Good news Bible*. Bangalore: Bible Society of World. 2008. Print.

Brannon, Linda. *Gender-Psychological Perspectives*. Boston: Library of Congress Cataloging-in-Publication Data, 1999. Print.

Dattani, Mahesh. *Collected Plays*. Vol. I. New Delhi: Penguin Books, 2000. Print.

Dhawan, R.K. and Tanu Pant. *The Plays of Mahesh Dattani—A Critical Response*. New Delhi: Prestige Books, 2005. Print.

Engels, Frederick. *The Origin of the Family, Private Property and the State*. Peking: Foreign Languages Press, 1978. Print.

Marx, Karl and Frederick Engels. *Manifesto of Communist Party*. USSR: Progress Publishers, 1972. Print.

10

Usage of Dolls by Mahesh Dattani and Girish Karnad

Jasmine Dordi

Franz Kafka once said in a letter;

> If the book we are reading does not wake us, as with a fist hammering on our skull, why then do we read it?.... What we must have are those books which come upon us like ill fortune, and distress us deeply, like the death of one we love better than ourselves.... A book must be an ice axe to break the sea frozen inside us. (qtd. in Barnet 82)

The aforementioned quote aptly suits the plays of Mahesh Dattani and Girish Karnad for their repertoire of plays is replete with an array of contemporary topics which are often a taboo. The plays of these two mavericks typically revolve around social causes and issues like women sexuality, incest and child abuse.

Mahesh Dattani and Girish Karnad occupy a very distinct and illustrious place in the realm of Indian drama in English. These avant-garde playwrights have given a new impetus to the Indian English Drama. While Girish Karnad uses myths, folklores and history to present the image of the present, Mahesh Dattani's plays showcase the mean ugly and unhappy aspects of the human life, through unconventional subjects. Both the writers present the nuances of drama so beautifully for they are actors, directors, writers rolled into one.

Feminine issues and the female angst form the crux of the plays *Hayavadana* and *Thirty Days in September.* While Girish

Karnad has depicted the yearning for perfection and ideal man that Padmini craves for, Dattani presents the pathos and the passion of a young vulnerable girl Mala who is sexually abused by her own maternal uncle.

Hayavadana, a Brechtian kind of play, is a remarkably enigmatic and trend setting play which primarily explores the struggle between the body and the mind for dominance of one over the other. It is a play that captivatingly incorporates motifs from traditional theatre—dolls, masks and the inversion of mock heroic mores. In the play Karnad cleverly grafts eleventh century Indian fable from Somadeva's *Kathasaritsagar* with Thomas Mann's story *The Transposed Heads*.

The play *Thirty Days in September*, cleft into three acts, is a tragic tale of a child's sexual abuse. The play was first performed at the Prithvi Theatre, Mumbai on 31st May, 2001. The play was commissioned by RAHI, a support group for women survivors of incest. Lillete Dubey observes;

> *Thirty Days in September* has touched hearts and consciences everywhere. Sensitive and powerful without ever offending sensibilities, it manages to bring home the horror and the pain within the framework of a very identifiable mother-daughter relationship. (Dattani 4)

Dattani dramatizes the issue of child sexual abuse and its repercussions on an individual's psyche. The gamut of incestuous relationships makes the story more heartrending. The play portrays the issue of incest through Mala and her mother, Shanta. Both the mother and the daughter are sexually molested in their infancy by the same person Vinay, who is Shanta's own brother. The sexual molestation affects both of the victims differently as one is browbeaten into bearing it silently due to social pressure and taboos and the other revolts against it. The play lays its foundation on the ordeal of Mala, who subsists with the torturing and mentally punishing memories of her abused past. The molester who is surprisingly her uncle subconsciously resides with her all the time as a stained reflection of the past, confines her natural growth and holds her back from pursuing her love interest exceeding the ominous thirty days period.

The plays are path breaking and both use the indigenous device of puppets with consummate skill. The dolls are mediums of revelation as they highlight the pathos hidden deep within the central characters' psyche. Hence they are at once symbols and theatrical metaphors. Plays like *A Doll's House* by Henrik Ibsen and *Cloud 9* by Churchill have used dolls to represent women and their powerlessness. Churchill uses an actual doll as an extremely significant stage prop to enhance the gravity of sexual inequality and homosexuality. Ibsen uses dolls as a metaphor to represent women in the Victorian era and how they lived alongside men, like dolls in *A Doll's House* which the masculine owned. Freud in his essay *The Uncanny* quotes, in relation to dolls, the German psychiatrist, Ernst Anton Jentsch's observation;

> ...that a particularly favourable condition for awakening uncanny feelings is created when there is intellectual uncertainty whether an object is alive or not, and when an inanimate object becomes too much like an animate one. (Rhy xi)

While the dolls in *Hayavadana* have verbal communication and have an opinion the doll of *Thirty Days in September* is mute yet ironically more vocal. Though the dolls in both the plays are minor characters yet important to the overall understanding of the plays. In Dattani's play the doll appears only in the stage directions yet its uncanny presence can be felt throughout. In *Hayavadana t*he dolls appear in just one act yet they play a significant role and help us understand the central character of Padmini.

In *Where I Live* Tennessee Williams describes his plays as relying on "metaphorical ways of expression" (Williams 146). He also says that "symbols are nothing but the natural speech of drama [...] the purest language of plays" (Williams 66). Dattani and Karnad use the metaphor of dolls to represent their feminine characters and how they are tied up and man-handled by the puppeteer, who in this case are the male characters.

Karnad uses the dolls as a Brechtian technique along with Bhagvata and Female Chorus to create the effect of alienation. Dattani on the other hand uses dolls as a symbol along with magazines, crossed dates on the calendar that are symbolic of Mala's past. The symbol of doll at a cursory glance may appear as merely a stage device, but it is not so. It represents and mimics Mala's psychological state. The doll is a recurring symbol that represents the unhealable wounds brought about by the loss of innocence and purity. Dattani draws parallels between Mala and the doll to present the guilt and the turmoil that Mala harbours in herself whereby she is synonymous of the ragged doll introduced early in the play.

In Act One 1 the stage direction mentions:

> ...we see the back of a life sized doll of seven-year- old girl propped on a chair. During the first conversation we only see the back of the head. With every subsequent taped conversation we see more of the profile. We only see the doll's full face after Deepak's taped conversation. (7-8)

During the first conversation of Mala with the psychiatrist we see only the back of the head. This clearly establishes the relationship between Mala and the doll. It is significant that the doll is of seven years of age—the age at which Mala is molested by her maternal uncle also that only the back of her head is revealed for Dattani gradually reveals the antecedent action of Mala's harrowing past. At the commencement of the play Mala like the doll hides herself under the veil for she says:

> Today is the 30th September...2001, and my name is (reverberate 'name is'.) I don't think I was to say my name.... I am sorry (Reverberate 'sorry'.) I am unsure about this...and a lot of other things. But this.... This is the first time you see that I...(reverberate 'first time'.) I know it is all my fault really...(reverberate 'my fault' almost till the end of the tape.) it must be. I must have asked for it.... Somehow I just seem to be made for it. Maybe I was born that way, may be.... This is what I was meant for. It is not anybody's fault, except my own. Sometimes I wish that my mother.... I am sorry but.... (9)

The uncanny presence of Doll pervades the play for even when it is not visible, we feel its presence. As in Act II, "The Doll is not visible in this scene, and there is no black out during Mala's voice on tape except at the end" (33), the focus of the light is not on the Doll and thus it is not highlighted to the audience. Just after this stage direction in a poignant monologue, Mala reveals a small fraction of the scars that her father's indifference towards her which have been inflicted on her. "...My father left us, for another woman.... I feel if I were more lovable he would have atleast visited us.... We continue to get money from him every month, and he pays the rent...but I haven't seen him in fifteen years.... I...don't think my mother and he got along-that way. Again, because of me..." (33). This clearly shows that her uncle had deeply imprinted on her psyche that she is responsible for the incest.

"The light comes up on the Doll once again" (34). The light that is focused on the Doll just after the soliloquy of Mala exemplifies that Mala herself is merely like a doll in the hands of a puppeteer who holds the string (in this case the uncle):

> My uncle just went away. He left me. He said he was disgusted with me—my behaviour. He never returned.... But now he is coming back. He is coming home. Please understand he is not a bad person or anything like that... I am so confused, I don't know what I feel for him...I know you are not supposed to tell me what I am to do, I am to figure that out for myself right? (34)

The dolls play a vital dramatic role. The function of the doll in Dattani is to act as a physical embodiment of the assault that Mala has been subjected to. The deep relationship between the Doll and Mala that exists throughout is brought out more significantly in the denouement. "The Doll's face is fully visible now. We cannot see the Doll's face, just its ragged limbs. The dress on the Doll is lifted and pinned at the Doll's forehead. The doll remains lit throughout the following scene" (45). The doll is fully visible now because the past of her sexual abuse is revealed to the readers. The dress of the doll is lifted and pinned at the dolls forehead is symbolic of her molestation and the fact that

Mala was treated as a doll fit "Only for this.... Only for this" (44) as Vinay says during the sexual act.

In Girish Karnad's *Hayavadana* the dolls are used for the dual purpose, testifying to the playwright's awareness of a large matrix of non-western indigenously Indian theatre entrenched in our ancient dramas as well as being symbolic.

In *Hayavadana*, Karnad makes use of ancient myth to interpret this old-age human dilemma of incompleteness and quest for identity and perfection. Through the play he presents the pictures of human beings in search of perfection and completeness and the play presents as many as four characters—Devdatta, Padmini, Hayavadana and Kapila, who are incomplete and who are consciously or unconsciously striving for the illusive ideal of perfection.

Karnad, through the use of dolls, reveals very carefully the thought processes and inner psyche of Padmini as she visualizes the gradual conversion of Devadatta's body into its original form and dreams of Kapila's strong body. Karnad explores Padmini's inner psyche by using two Doll characters. Since her consciousness is divided between the two aspects of body and mind that she yearns, therefore, the playwright ingeniously divides the dolls also into Doll I and Doll II.

Freud says, "the interpretation of dreams is the royal road to knowledge of the unconscious activities of the mind" (Welsh 4) and helps in understanding the diverse facets of the persona. In *Hayavadana* it is the dolls which see and narrate Padmini's dream about Kapila, revealing the illicit desires she feels but cannot express as a married woman.

In Padmini's reveries, the dolls see a man other than her husband.

> Doll I: Look
>
> Doll II: Where?
>
> Doll I: Behind her eyelids. She is dreaming.
>
> Doll II: I don't see anything.
>
> Doll I: It's hazy—hasn't started yet. Do you see it now?
>
> Doll II (eagerly): Yes, Yes.

(They stare at her.)

Doll I: A man.

Doll II: But not her husband. (160)

The dolls are also the doppelganger of Padmini. They report Devadutta's transformation. When he touches Doll I it feels the change and says:

> Doll I: His palms! They were rough when he first brought us here like a labourer's but now they are soft, sickly soft like a young girl's.
>
> Doll II: I know. I've noticed something too.
>
> Doll I: What?
>
> Doll II: His stomach. It was tight and muscular. Now....
>
> Doll I: I know it's soft and loose. (158)

When Doll I calls the hands of Devadutta sickly soft it is uncannily the opinion of Padmini that they project. The fact that the dolls speak immediately after Padmini notices the subtle changes in the body of her husband is also significant.

The split in Padmini's psyche, and the fact that the dolls represent her consciousness becomes prominent when, the dolls start quarrelling with each other. The dolls represent her insurmountable chasm that she is teetering upon as she is utterly unable to choose between Devadutta and Kapila.

Though she tries hard to find happiness with the perfect Devadutta she has created, once Devadutta's body changes back to its original self she once again yearns for Kapila. The dolls share with the audience the lies and the subterfuge and the handsome stranger who visits her dreams.

In both the plays apart from the symbolic significance that the dolls have, the gestures, the position of the dolls is equally significant. The language of the play broadly conceived includes the costumes that the characters wear, the gestures that the characters make. The costume and gestures of the dolls have been cleverly contrived by the two playwrights.

In *Thirty Days in September* the fact that the doll is present at the office of the psychiatrist is noteworthy because it signifies

Mala's journey from being a doll to a woman who is capable of loving. The doll symbol is effective—corresponds with the idea of numbness or silence which Shanta maintains against victimization of herself and her daughter. It also symbolizes that Mala is not permitted to express reality to society.

In drama, symbolism is considered as the reaction and style of acting and the doll's reaction of lifting the skirt and covering her eyes could imply the sexual act and the shame it feels during the act. The ragged limbs connote the bruises and the tainted memories that Mala carries with her. The position of the doll at the end facing Mala is also symptomatic because Mala has finally confronted the past and realized that it was not her fault.

It is now that she finally confronts her uncle for destroying her soul, "Fifteen minutes of my summer holidays, add them up. Fifteen minutes multiplied by thirty or thirty-one or whatever. That's how long or how little it took for you to send me to hell for the rest of my life!"(53).

Gestures too are a part of the language of drama, and one of the most revealing gestures of Mala that is highly symbolic is "Mala picks up the doll finally with care, smoothens its dress and comforts it" (58). This reveals that she has been healed, psychologically and emotionally and is now ready to step out of the internal detestation and fear she had due to her past.

In *Hayavadana,* the dolls allow Karnad to introduce the voice of the society into an otherwise three-character story. The dolls remind the spectators of the social mores of the society and of propriety. But the dolls have a dark side too. They are gossipy and judgmental, like nosey neighbours. They are important because they remind spectators of the presence of the society—and of propriety. Even their typical attires are discreet codes within themselves. It is noteworthy that they are wrapped in such a way that it makes the reader ponder upon the decryption of their sex which connotes that morality has no gender.

> Doll I: ...dressed in silk....
>
> Doll II: ...seated on a cushion shelf....
>
> Doll I: ...given new clothes every week.... (155)

Dolls are repeatedly used as motifs by these two stalwarts of post-independent era to add extended connotations and give the readers better insight into the central character. Dattani's mute doll paradoxically represents the tumultuous silent agony of Mala and Shanta, while Karnad's dolls to the contrary are garrulous to the extreme and bring forth the constraints of a society for a woman.

Works Cited

Barnet, Sylvan. *A Short Guide to Writing about Literature*. New York: Harper Collins, 1996. Print.

Dattani, Mahesh. *Collected Plays: Screen, Stage and Radio Plays*. Volume Two. New Delhi: Penguin, 2005: Print. The figures in brackets pertaining to *Thirty Days in September* are from this source.

Karnad, Girish. *Collected Plays*. Volume One. New Delhi: Oxford University Press, 2005. Print. The figures in brackets pertaining to Hayavandana are from this source.

Rhy, Jean. *Wide Sargasso Sea*. New Delhi: Penguin, 2000. Print.

Welsh, Alexander. FREUD'S *Wishful Dream Book*. New Jersey: Priceton University Press, 1994: Print.

Williams, Tennessee. *Where I Live: Selected Essays*. New York: New Directions, 1978. Print.

11

The Sense of Time in *Thirty Days in September* and *The Girl Who Touched the Stars*

Vimmie Manoj

The word *drama* derives from a Greek word meaning "to do," and thus drama is usually related with the idea of action. Drama is a fictional or real story about events in the lives of characters. A drama comprises twelve core elements inclusive of Focus, Tension, Timing, Rhythm, Contrast, Mood, Space Language, Sound, Symbol, Conflict and Climax (Justin Cash). The Playwright may use these elements in any phase of the act and in an order as per his/her choice bringing in individuality to the play. Mahesh Dattani is a prominent name in the list of Playwrights in English; he has won the 1998 Sahitya Akademi Award for his contribution for English Drama in India. *Tara, Final Solution, On a Muggy Night in Mumbai, Seven Steps around the Fire, Brief Candle, Thirty Days in September* and *The Girl Who Touched the Stars, Where Did I Leave My Purdah, The Big Fat City* are some of his prominent plays. Themes like social probes, communal tensions, and gender discrimination, consumerism, homosexuality and child abuse are candidly dealt by him. Mahesh Dattani intricately uses the time technique in tandem with the core elements. His plays not only deal with the material aspect instead added with the element of Time they change and bring motion to the flow. The paper focuses on the sense of time in his two plays *Thirty Days in September* and *The Girl Who Touched the Stars*.

Taking into consideration the chronological importance of Time correlating with the contemporary magnitude where the Relativity concept in the field of Physics (1905-16) focuses on the three-dimensional Space and Time as a separate identity, it specifies that the Time interval between events is not absolute instead a relative to the way of looking at them. Philosophers like Samuel Alexander and Henri Bergson hypothesize that the basic aspect of reality is Space-Time. Samuel Alexander assumes it as a 'matrix' or 'stuff of things' from which facets of reality like matter, life, mind and Deity emerge. Henri Bergson describes it as a 'duration' from which the facets of consciousness, matter, time and evolution evolve (Subramanyam 130). However, these philosophical inquiries produced a new outlook among writers whose prime concern was to deal with character or personality inside a literary creation. The Naturalists accounted Space and Time as separate entities and held the separation of mind and the external events as final. They thus never aimed to penetrate beneath the surface and appeared satisfied with the presentation of the objective reality. The Bloomsbury Group writers like Virginia Woolf and Joyce rejected the division between the real and the virtual and advocated that the human mind can be assumed to relive past events. According to them the events in external life—the spatial aspect and the external events may spread over a long period of time, yet these events leave impressions which may be recalled over a very short duration. Dr S. Radhakrishnan points out that according to Bergson "true life is not growing self which goes on gathering its past experience through memory pressing forward to its future progress...it is undivided present to which the categories of Time are irrelevant" (Radhakrishnan 141). One can therefore assume that in a human mind the past impinges on the time present and both look to future time because the mind does not categorize the past, present and the future. Virginia Woolf in her essay on *Modern Fiction* comments taking into consideration the concept of time and space:

> Life is not a series of gig lamps symmetrically arranged; life is a luminous halo, a semi-transparent envelope

> surrounding us from the beginning of consciousness to the end. (Woolf)

Awareness of reality is the state of man's mind where the mind can be accounted as being a myriad of impressions during a particular time. Mahesh Dattani wrote the play *Thirty Days in September* after being commissioned by RAHI to write a play on child abuse. His other play *The Girl Who Touched the Stars* is a radio play inspired by the life of Kalpana Chawla. In both the plays, *Thirty Days in September* and *The Girl Who Touched the Stars* the sense of time is followed.

The play *Thirty Days in September* is divided in three Acts. The sense of time and space can be examined by analyzing the conversations between the four characters, Mala, Deepak, Shanta and The Man in the play.

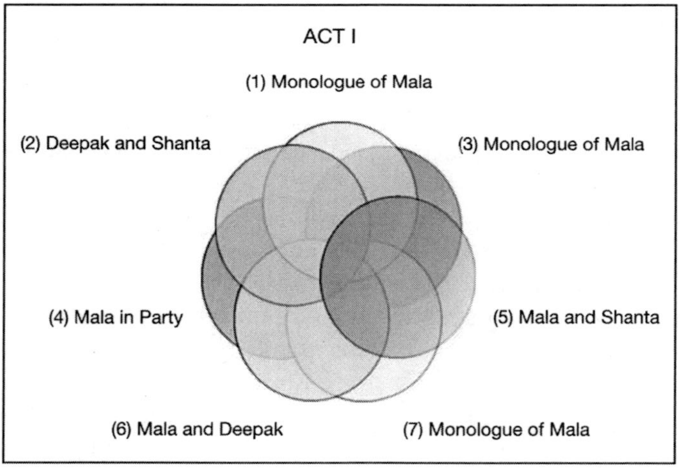

It can be analyzed that Dattani uses the consciousness narrative technique to illustrate the countless thoughts and feelings which pass through the human mind. In his contemporary style Dattani uses Mala's taped conversation addressed to an empty chair of the counselor as a monologue of Mala in the play *Thirty Days in September,* Act I, to portray her thought process. Characterized by associative leaps in thought and lack of punctuation the monologue highlights the struggle and restlessness of Mala. It associates some error of the past that will lead to a conflicting climax of future.

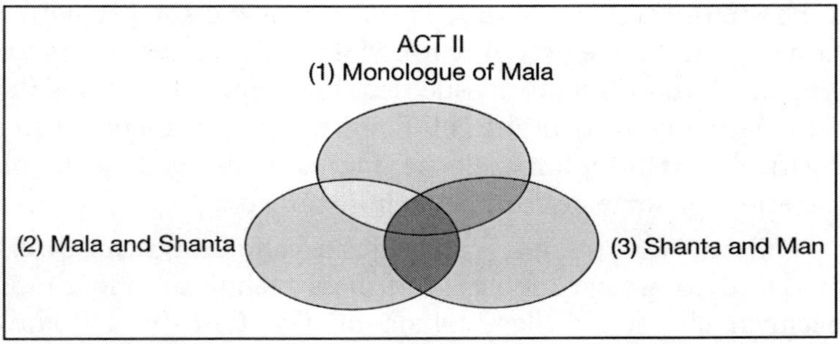

The conflict between the two characters is reached to its peak at the end of Act II. Dattani allows the reader to anticipate the outcome in the plot and succeeds in building the tension in Act II.

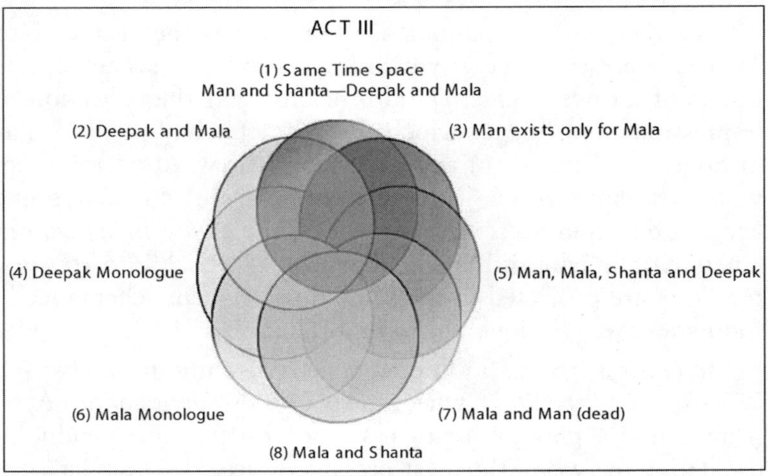

In Act III the confusion is highlighted with many scenes being played simultaneously. The climax is reached and at the end of the Act III, the conflict is settled. Throughout the three acts the mood is created through a combination of several dramatic and stagecraft elements. For example the taped monologues, light effects, background music and with two scenes played simultaneously without dimming or raising lights set up a mood wherein all these elements work in perfect harmony with each other. The two parallel conversations in the opening of the Act III between Man-Shanta and Deepak-Mala focus on the complexity of the situation and emotions. The catharsis is displayed with the act when the Man exists only for Mala in her conversation with Deepak. Dattani receptively succeeds in scripting the sordid issue of the sexually abused girl child and the pain displayed can be sensitively felt bringing in goose bumps while reading the play (the effect of stage act can be well imagined).

Dattani warps and wefts the psychoanalytical threads interlaced to weave the consciousness technique. He chooses specimen characters like Bhavna in *The Girl Who Touched the Stars* while Mala and Shanta in *Thirty Days in September,* who represent the dominant impressions and those stored up in their consciousness. Dattani creates a juxtaposition of what is happening and what has happened (the flashback).

Another *modus operandi* Dattani uses is the segments of Time. He presets Time at which impressions are schemed, like points of diffused lights. Dattani reconstructs the collection of impressions and images which the character had at particular instants or fragments of time, working backward on the time-scale. The impressions in the consciousness of characters like Mala and Shanta in Act III scene 1 of *Thirty Days in September* and that of Bhavna and Young Bhavna in *The Girl Who Touched the Stars* are projected in the same time segment schematically following the technique of 'Foreshortening'.

In contrast to the traditional style is his radio play *The Girl Who Touched the Stars,* where the play is not divided into Acts. Instead it is a play on a single string with the time pendulum oscillating between the past-present-future. As Bhavna says "Future. Past. It's all the same now. As random as our thoughts" (73). Every instant the Time zone changes from Present to Past or Present to Future; the sound either of lullaby or TV news broadcast is used. As Tracey Neale puts it in that Radio plays have the ability to take you into a world of imagination where one cannot see the picture instead it is all in the head of the listener (53). Technically Dattani has worked very aptly in creating the contrast in the Time zones.

Working on the mechanism of Time, Dattani uses symbols to suggest some significant experience in the past, leaving indelible impressions. However, symbols in drama may be unrestricted since the symbol can be varied or diverted depending upon its context and function in a scene. Thus symbolic association in drama may not be always essential or regular and perpetually depends on the playwright's selection of the core element. Literary symbols in drama may be an object, action, gesture, or dialogue that is important to the play, depending on its description or occurrence. Its reoccurrence may occur at a climactic or significant moment in the play. It is important to note that not all objects used in the play can be considered as a symbol. One needs to cross-examine the object that appears in the context of its original connect or as a representative symbol, its repetitive occurrence or use of symbol as a connective between acts.

The reoccurrence and timing of the lullaby in his play *The Girl Who Touched the Stars* produces a reverberating effect that brings into the sharp contrast with the voices in the cockpit, a method adopted by Dattani to show the contrast between the present and the past. In the beginning the lullaby is associated with the flashback and the play oscillates in the time zone swinging from present to future via the past. The single character of Bhavna is split into two, the young Bhavna an aspiring young astronaut, Bhavna—the future of the young girl. As the play proceeds unveiling the plot of how the young Bhavna becomes a woman "Looking down at the world" (71). Bhavna's mother tricks her father for five years hiding her identity as a baby girl, instead christens her as a boy Bhuvan. The play is about the journey of young Bhavna, initially as Bhuvan, a hidden identity and unwanted girl child to the rebellious Bhavna who wants to fulfill her dream of touching the stars and which she eventually fulfills. The use of lullaby 'Chanda Mama' is heard in the background repetitively to add to the time effect in the play. The lullaby with the words calling the moon as the uncle is symbolic on two planes, first it connects with the dreamy world of the girl child and secondly the stark reality that threatens the existence of women in society. In the later part of the play the lullaby is synchronized with the dialogues pointing to the interplay of the past and the future finally fusing in the present. The same play has the act of young Bhavna climbing the mango tree and it becomes a symbolic act of the adult Bhavna reach the space as the astronaut, "The earth is one big mango tree and I am on top of it" (77). The reoccurrence of her blood being spilled on the earth correlates with the past event of her school days. Dattani thus succeeds in technically using the symbols to their fullest panorama so that they become quite an intricate part of the play. The symbolic adaptation in the play explores the flux faced by a woman who clings to the veracity of the present yet her past drags her back forcing her to face the challenges of her being.

Taking into account the aspect whether the symbol is hidden or described elaborately by the writer, one can agree that certain symbols like that of the Doll and the portrait of Lord Krishna have been elaborately described by Dattani in his play *Thirty Days in September.* The play opens with the life-sized doll of a seven-year-old girl propped up on a chair. Props are the easiest to work with because objects in everyday life are symbols in society. Initially only the back of her head is visible and with each taped conversation (monologue) more of the doll's profile is disclosed adding to the development of suspense. The doll's full face is seen after Deepak's taped monologue in *Act III.* "The doll is fully visible now. We cannot see the doll's face, just ragged limbs. The dress on the doll is lifted and pinned on to the doll's forehead" (125). The plot unfolds further as "Mala breaks away from Deepak and lies on the bed, taking her T-shirt over her head..." (124). Here the prop symbol of doll is superimposed as Mala. Later in the same Act, "The Man walks to the doll and picks it up, holding the doll by its skirt so that the skirt covers the dolls face. He rocks the doll while he speaks" (137). At the end of the act when Mala stabs the Man to death "Mala picks up the doll, smoothens its dress and comforts it" (138). Alike the poet Rainer Maria Rilke, Dattani shows that the doll besides being a symbolic representation of the human body, it also symbolizes a sexual/erotic signification. Using the prop of doll symbolically Dattani points that women are viewed as objects that have no realistic value. Although the modern society may be reticent yet the doll reminds that masochism is still familiar and present. Dattani uses the fact that psychoanalysts have worked with children to discuss dolls in the context of play therapy, where they, like other toys, allow the child to project unconscious processes and facilitate the resolution of conflicts which the child is unable to articulate (Erik Erikson). Hence the symbolic representation of the doll in the play implies a greater meaning than the literal suggestion. The doll becomes the link between the past and present Time zone.

In the same play Dattani uses the picture of Lord Krishna as a symbol. In the living room of Shanta and Mala has dominantly positioned "a large picture of Shri Krishna" (87). Shanta often turns to the portrait and avoids Mala, "simply trying to escape as always" (102). Shanta's statement that she has put herself at the feet of the God shows her inaction. Mala troubled by her silence and inaction flings the painting out of the door and Shanta reacts re-entering with the portrait and the pieces of glass on the portrait. She remains silent hoping her God would "send his Sudarshan Chakra to defend you, to defend us from the demon inside you, not outside you" (108). Dattani propels to reach a contrast in Act III when Mala accuses Shanta of ignoring her pain "fifteen minutes when he was destroying my soul...you were praying, your eyes avoiding mine" (133). Shanta prefers to remain silent "I remained silent not because I wanted to, but I didn't know how to speak…I looked at Him…I am dumb" (135). After disclosing herself as a victim of sexual abuse herself, Shanta picks up pieces of glass from the portrait and jabs them in her mouth. She turns dumb and finds peace with herself as symbolic as her name 'Shanta' meaning peace. The play closes with Shanta praying to God and the only sound she makes is the ringing of the bell. Dattani uses the mythological symbol of Shri Krishna, where Shanta awaits his arrival to save her and her daughter Mala from exploitation as God had saved Draupadi from the abuse. He has cleverly linked the present struggle of both Shanta and Mala to survive with the myth of Draupadi as in the Indian epic the *Mahabharata*. The sense of Time is intricately woven around the symbols in such a way that the metaphorical device shows a comparison between the actual identity and the abstract idea. Thus in the Time zone, alike the characters, the symbols too have a propensity to become powerful. Dattani succeeds in imparting symbolical importance to a particular detail such that it leaps beyond the literal action, dialogue or time space into a symbolic interpretation connoted to its interpretive connection.

Conclusively, the study of Mahesh Dattani's plays validates him as an authentic contemporary playwright. He uses Time techniques to maneuver a continuous parallel between the contemporary and antiquity such that whilst his plays are rooted in contemporary urban experience yet they have a significance which can travel beyond boundaries. The treatment of his depiction of characters and situations, technical treatment, dramatic elements and the sociological issues are inspirational and undoubtedly universal in appeal.

Works Cited

Commom Reader, I Series, 1925. Print.

Dattani, Mahesh. *Brief Candle Three Plays: The Girl Who Touched the Stars: A Radio Play.* New Delhi: Penguin Books, 2010. Print. All textual citations are from this edition.

———. *Brief Candle Three Plays: Thirty Days in September.* New Delhi: Penguin Books, 2010. Print. All textual citations are from this edition.

Erikson, Erik. *Childhood and Society* (New York, 1950), hereafter cited in text as *CS*; Melanie Klein, *Narrative of a Child Analysis* (New York, 1961); Bruno Bettelheim, *The Uses of Enchantment* (New York, 1975). Print.

http://www.thedramateacher.com/dramatic-elements/ Justin Cash. Web.

Radhakrishnana, S. *An Idealist View of Life.* Allen Publications, 1957. Print.

Subramanyam, N.S. *Movements in Modern English Novels.* Gwalior: Kitab Ghar, 1967. Print.

12

Of Scripts and Movies

Bandana Burman

If a script were like garlands and the flowers—the Movies, then indeed Mahesh Dattani is a master craftsman of garlands most exquisite. Because,

> Movies touch our hearts and engage our vision.
> And change the way we see things.
> They take us to other planes
> They open doors and minds.
> Movies are the memories of our lifetime....
>
> Martin Scorsese

But all movies and plays must of necessity entertain and for this purpose be cohesively collated. The entertainment bit is irrevocably intertwined with the plot which in its turn provides the thread of thematic continuity. For a plot to be successful says the Natya Shashtra, it must encompass bhava or mood, raga or melodic framework and taal or rhythm. In modern times, drama no longer holds sway over the masses as it did in the past. However, that is not to say that dramatic content is now passé, as drama today, has resurged in the vibrant new avatar of movies and the success of a movie relies seminally on its script.

Any visual medium be it a movie or a play must be based on a contemporary script to garner its audiences' attention. Mahesh Dattani understands that pretty well. This pre-eminent writer and director of scripts is renowned for his sensitive handling and portrayal of issues which others of a lesser calibre would normally trivialize or reduce to a ham handed comic farce. Besides this, there is another aspect to the redoubtable Dattani and that is that he is also a consummate artist, who effortlessly gets under and into the skin of the characters that he is writing about to trenchantly portray their compromise filled lives. The movie *Ek Alag Mausam* which was scripted by him is a perfect case study.

At the turn of this century, world cinema saw the emergence of four excellent movies that dealt with the spectre of H.I.V. These were *An Early Frost, My Brother Nikhil, Phir Milenge* and *Ek Alag Mausam.* The unifying factor of all the four is not just their theme of AIDS but also the fact that they usurp the spectators' reality by surprise. All of these four movies are single-handedly united in their unstinting support of the subaltern or the underling, in this case the HIV positives. What differs in each of these movies and scripts is the telling of the tale.

Directed by John Erman, *An Early Frost* was a path breaking film in the eighties and it paved the way for later masterpieces like *Philadelphia, Go Towards the Light, The Littlest Victims* and *The Ryan White Story*. For its subject matter it has Aidan Quinn play the dashing and gay young lawyer Michael Pierson who is devastated on discovering that he has AIDS. This too at a time when people really didn't know much about the disease and to have a gay male protagonist was simply too over the top to say the least.

The beauty of this particular movie however is that it provides an incisive view into the schismatic dissidence of insurmountable proportions that occurs between Pierson and the rest of the world, including even his family, when the ugly secret becomes known. Naturally what follows in his life is immense and sheer personal trauma as he seethes under the varying degrees of ostracism and slander that his kith and kin put him through, utterly non-cognizant as they are of the relevance of his desperation.

Of course, *'An Early Frost'*—is an out and out tear jerker but it is also at the same time an absolutely non-pedantic, non-carping, sensitive and reassuring movie. Indeed it is cathartic too as it takes its viewers on an emotional journey that traverses the vast panorama of intense and immense psychological suffering which finally ends in compassion and acceptance.

'My Brother Nikhil', on the other hand, begins with angst and evolves from there. This poignant tale is narrated by a sister and it revolves around her brother Nikhil, who suffers from AIDS. The narrator eschews nothing and bares all. She delves deep into Nikhil's psyche and ekes out the sadness, betrayal and frustration felt by the protagonist. It is only posthumously that the family which had shunned him in life, reconciles to his suffering .the common denominator in both these movies is the suffering undergone by all involved.

Phir Milenge is once again a movie that deals with the concept of AIDS. It has been directed by the South Indian actress Revathi and has Shilpa Shetty playing the main protagonist. Revathi was spurred on to direct this film by her conscience because it went against the grain for her to stand by and watch society doom the HIV infected persons to a living death. She amps up the watchability factor of *'Phir Milenge'* tremendously with her sensitive portrayal of the main female protagonist, Tamanna Sahni. Tamanna is a gutsy young lass, swinging her way into the professional stratosphere of a reputed advertising firm, under the aegis of a father like CEO. But life throws her a googly when Salman Khan re-enters her life for a short but impassioned tryst and then moves on.

Shilpa as Tamanna, carries on her life sadder but wiser and (unbeknownst to her) also infected by the Human Immunodeficiency Virus. Knowledge of the disease very naturally makes all those who had previously welcomed her with open arms, shun her to the point of ostracism. Naturally our protagonist finds herself getting beleaguered day by day in every way, till one bleak day not is she just down and out on her luck but also jobless to boot.

Refusing to take it all lying down Tamanna actually gets going when the going gets tough and turns to the law for help. Our Galahad in disguise is the lawyer Tarun Anand (Abhishek Bachchan), who agrees to field her case after a bit of dithering and pussy footing. Naturally all ends well and she finally wins the case. *Phir Milenge* is overall a woman centric movie which is indeed praise worthy because it takes a close look at the ever changing ethical and moral mores of our social structure.

One of the rivetting themes of the kudos garnering '*Phir Milenge*' is the very sensitive portrayal of a woman's inner strength which can be brought to the fore by adverse circumstances. Yet in summation its strongest message however is that society has absolutely no right to stigmatize the HIV positives. For to do so is simply to deny them their fundamental right to a fruitful life—however so long as it might be.

Mahesh Dattani who is not known as a rebel playwright for nothing, took the same socially taboo subject, turned it around on its anvil and served it up as '*Ek Alag Mausam*,' with refreshing sangfroid. His mantra throughout the play, which was later made into a movie was, "is it too much to hope for that in his last few days they have that they learn to laugh, to think of their life. To seize the moment..." (Dattani 505) very bit of the script is undoubtedly about AIDS, but served in a typically Dattaniesque twist.

His protagonists know the writing on the wall and yet they dare to hope, to dream, to fall in love and most important is the message that Aids can happen to anyone—even an utter gentleman like George, who contacted it not by sexual philandering (Surprise! Surprise!) but after he, "...was seriously injured..., Joseph gave him blood. And—unknowingly—gave him the virus.' Joseph ironically was Dr. Machado's son" (Dattani 549) and then of course is the intrepid Dr. Machado, who keeps it all cohesively together with his own particular brand of wisdom. "...All lovers are fools. I will promise anything to save Jeevan Jyoti..." (Dattani 543). Mahesh Dattani—the evergreen script writer—is famous not just for his interesting characters and intriguing plots but also for the fact that drama forms the plinth and the background for all his scripts and plays. Dattani combines and collates all of the above with compassion cohesively, without a single jarring incident.

The central theme of his outstanding, *Ek Alag Mausam*, revolves around several ideas. It includes the hospice which is appropriately named Jeevan Jyoti; a budding romance between two of its main HIV infused protagonists, Aparna and George. It would not be amiss to state here that Aparna sadly is a divorcee with a past where she was forced to terminate her pregnancy because her philandering husband had not thought it important to tell her that he was HIV positive. Hence when she meets George, little does she know that they are destined to find romantic completeness. Apt indeed in her case are the following lines by Herbert Shipman:

> Across the gateway of my heart I wrote "No thoroughfare"
> But love came laughing by, and cried:
> I enter everywhere.

Finally of course are also the abandoned children who are also being fostered at Jeevan Jyoti by irrepressible Dr. Machado. Perusal of the play brings home to the reader the fact that the hoi polloi and the bourgeoisie are not beneath his attention, in fact it is actually quite the reverse. These then are the characters whose inner dimensions and psychological ticklings, he seeks to portray.

Dattani knows exactly what he wants to say through the medium of the script and without either trivializing the issue or compromising the gravitas of the situation at hand. It is a fact universally accepted that a good scriptwriter is like a magician because he effortlessly turns around hackneyed concepts and presents old wine in a brand new avatar. Indian cinema thrives on melodrama and the best way to wring it out is through the theme of illness, but it takes a Mahesh Dattani (who is also a script writer extraordinaire) to take the concept and infuse it with dollops of rebelliousness and drama.

HIV and it's close relative AIDS are more often than not treated as an anathema at worst and an abomination at best. The need of the hour is an absolute turn about in the mind set of people at large. Movies are probably the best way to do so. Directors and script writers like Dattani, Onir and Revathi have attempted to take up the cudgels on the behalf of these intentionally marginalized group of HIV positive people, through the medium of movies because in the long run people need to be entertained and movies are what they invariably turn to. What better way than to serve up a movie that not just entertains but also educates with a view!

Works Cited

Dattani, Mahesh. *Collected Plays*—Volume Two, Screen Stage and Radio Plays. New Delhi: Penguin Books, 2005. Print. (The figures in brackets are from this source.)

Shipman, Herbert. Boardofwisdom.com/togo/quotes. Web.

13

Morning Raga: The Music of Life Epitomized

Nutan Kulshreshtha

As per the tradition of Hindustani classical music every *raga* has its own time to be sung or played. The *raga* is supposed to be more enthralling if its compatibility of time is maintained. Though any morning *raga* be it *Bhairavi* tends to become much more pleasing to ears but the one indicated through the screen play *Morning Raga* by Mahesh Dattani has a peculiar charm of its own. Its music pervades over the entire play from the beginning till the end sometime sweet sometime harsh and jarring. The music scape portrayed by Dattani depicts alternating worlds. According to Dattani himself, "It is about a meeting of two worlds", he explains: "A story that brings together the modern and the traditional, unites the past with the present, Carnatic music with Western music, fate and coincidence with individual choices."

The title along with its association with the world of music connotes a particular time that is morning as the most suitable one for the consummate presentation of the *raga* under consideration. The story rotates around Swarnalatha who lives in an anguished past. The very end of the play turns out to be sort of wish fulfillment on her part, though she is forcibly encouraged by one of the characters to sing it. Thus morning raga turns out to be the climax song sung by her. The story runs more like a hangover of the past because Swarnalatha holds herself guilty for the death of Vaishnavi, Abhinay's mother in an accident. The moment she finds Abhinay coming to her house, she feels apprehensive of him and suspects that he might have come to blame her for the death of his mother.

The story moves around mainly through three families and their surviving successors after a car-bus collision across a bridge. From the very beginning of the play the two worlds—that of village bus stand, Swarnalatha, her husband Mr. Shastri, their four-year-old child followed by Vaishnavi and her male child of about the same age, on one hand and the other world comprising Mr. and Mrs. Kapoor and their toddler girl are simultaneously depicted and are put to contrast as well.

There is a world of villagers scrambling for seats with their baggage, tamburi, violin, a world full of chatter and excitement; the driver praying to the picture of *Lord Ganesh*; the passengers singing and also a 'fair amount of noise from the bus'. It's here where the young kid of Vaishnavi is seen drawing a pattern of the sun on a dusty window pane. Still another world is depicted through the family of Mr. Kapoor outside a city home, with a briefcase Mr. Kapoor getting into his car. While driving he puts the stereo on playing some 'popular western number of the seventies', ironically enough fumbling for accessories like 'hip flask' and here 'a puff of smoke from his cigarette' clouds the frame.

Here the playwright makes a skilled alternation of the two words one is purely rural but rooted in nature while the other is urban and utterly artificial. Here the villagers, 'settle down and hold their children and their musical instruments closely', there 'Mrs. Kapoor pulls the daughter in and shuts the door even as Mr. Kapoor is getting into his car'. The dichotomy between the natural and rural versus the artificial and urban world is heightened as if the 'dusty window panes' of the bus mock at the clouds of cigarette puffs on the windscreen of the car. The young kid drawing the patterns heralds the final morning in the life of the protagonists which occurs in the end of the play.

As the bus moves at high speed with the happy faces of the children, their mothers and the musical instruments, the car approaching fast with stereo on collides. The disaster dawns when we see the violin case flowing gently down the river even as the music from the car plays on...'Fade out'. The music that should have greeted the glorious birth, a new life through bright rising sun recedes into a swan song of one generation. It is after twenty years, the young Abhinay, son of Vaishnavi is forced to get up at 8 a.m. by an alarm clock, representing the generation living in small apartments as slaves to electronic gadgets. His day begins with the music of computer keys and cell phones. The only common thing that seems to be linking the two generations is music but that too of an entirely different type. Here we have music created by the alarm clock singing 'rise and shine' with a long beep or the clinking sound caused accidentally by his throwing of the cell phone. He is in hurry. The first dialogue of the play, rather an elliptically broken monologue begins "Ya... shit" reflecting his disturbed state of mind.

We have some advertising jingle being played when Abhinay reaches an advertising company office to meet Rajeev who, as the director of recording company, is after some fine line and a singer. Long after this meeting we can grope into his wish.... He wants to start his own music band *Pratibimb*. The conversation between Rajeev with his pop succeeds in working out some nonsense Western type of note for which Abhinay feels like throttling him. Coincidentally this meeting ending in angst on the part of Abhinay leads to a village bus stand where he is seen last one to get off the bus.

Here we see a nice fusion of the two worlds. The city dweller comes back to his village home. The sprawling paddy fields, the old man, Appa Rau with his buffalo *Annapoorna* seem to give him a warm welcome. Against the screech of tyres, here we hear the buffalo mewing. But again life's music becomes harsh when Abhinay hears 'a tinkle of anklets and some hurried activity' from his widower father's room and feels annoyed with his father's dalliance. Abhinay's disrespect is reflected in his shifting of deceased mother's photograph to another room. Even his conversation with his father along the paddy fields clearly reveals his morose reaction. The natural landscape with crickets taking over the silence of the village palm trees parallels his inner turmoil. The picture of mother with a Carnatic Violin in hand accelerates his desire for having his own music band *Pratibimb*. His thoughts force him to hunt after his mother's Violin. The scene with Appa Rau cutting coarse jokes for his search giving a really practical advice "we forget all we want to forget. Why remember all that brings you pain?" and his funny attempts to delineate the origin and history of Carnatic Violin prove to be an utter failure to divert Abhinay from immense grief.

The next exterior of late morning by the riverside picturing the crow-feeding-ritual after the death of Abhinay's mother with its paraphernalia of rice balls etc. sets a contrasting view. Here on another spot other side the river, shows back of some woman (who tends to be Swarnalatha) washing her hands in the river. Her singing is interrupted by Abhinay's arrival and she stops singing and proceeds away. Seeing grown up Abhinay and the car clash she is left aghast. In fact Pinkee, an attractive young girl in her early twenties, unable to control the speed of the car and the stereo going on takes a sudden halt.

The riverside bridge, the car, the speed, the stereo, etc. all are sufficient accessories provoking in Swarnalatha's psyche a kaleidoscopic flashback of the bus car collision that occurred about twenty years back. She gives an apprehensive word of caution to Abhinay while Pinkie apologizes and shows her emotional concern for the probable hurt she might have caused to him. Abhinay stands still staring at the source of music. Noticing that it bothers Abhinay, she turns the stereo off.

An old woman from among the villagers witnessing this incident is driven back to the memories of past accident. She starts accusing Pinkie addressing Pinkie to be a male driver. What is curious to note in this event is that the event occurred immediately after Swarnalatha sang. In the past also the collision took place when she was going in a bus with her husband, young son, Vaibhavi and Abhinay long back. Although it was just a coincidence but it led her to the verge of sinking. Twenty years back her wish to give a vocal performance of some *raga* in South Indian style in which her friend Vaishnavi was going to accompany her on the Carnatic violin could not be fulfilled. May be this is why the hobgoblins of past haunt her present also. Whenever she turns to music the past accident flashes back to her.

Now the dramatic entry of Abhinay and Pinkie turns instrumental in bringing her back to sing. The two simultaneous exteriors run parallel—in one by the bridge is Pinkie, holding an umbrella for Abhinay and a bullock cart dragging Pinkie's Santro through the rain and the other one, picturing a part of the village with Swarnalatha walking through rain in a daze. She faints and a glass of water is offered to her. A little girl who tugs at her mother's sari is told that the old woman (Swarnalatha) could not take care of her child. May be in a state of stupor it hurts her so much so that now she decides to appease Abhinay somehow to balance for the death of her own son Madhav.

A little bit of familiarity develops between Pinkie and Abhinay and the girl who did her Mass Communication is told the plans of Abhinay "I composed jingles for some stupid commercials, now.... I want to start a music group." The moment the girl learns about the accident with Abhinay's mother and the consequent emotional shocks that he undergoes now, she offers herself to sing for his band and thereby to compensate for the accident that partially injured Abhinay. They drive along the city and in a cafe see 'a college kid is jamming away on his guitar and singing ...with hand banging motions throwing his hair back and forth'. Abhinay is inspired to ask him regarding the guitar. Reaching the college they also enjoy music by nodding their heads to the beats of a drummer who is a bald, tattooed, huge, bare chested, muscular guy."

As both Abhinay and Pinkie smile in approval, the drummer stops and boasts of a bulky sum if they want him to play in their music band. Waving him good bye "Sorry we are a bit low of friends" they proceed ahead in search of accompanists for the music band. In a next cut they are shown reaching the home of an elderly man who strums a guitar and are received warmly. This search for the music band also takes them to a man with a guitar, staring at a vulgar looking poster.

His act of watching the obscene poster is hindered by Pinkie's comment who just appreciates him for playing the guitar. They invite this Munna who is "wiry and meek looking, wearing rounded spectacles, a clean white starched shirt and a sober grey pants" to join. Their search initially culminates in Abhinay's buying a set of drums from music store owned by Balaji who feels proud of calling himself Bals. Finally all three reach with drum set, key board, etc. at Mrs. Kapoor's Boutique to carry on with their practice.

Both the protagonists Swarnalatha the female and Abhinay the male are shown involved in music in some way or the other. The worlds to which they belong are entirely different. Swarnalatha's world is of grown up mature individuals who prefer south Indian classical music with tamburi and Carnatic violin, with bordered saris and villagers while that of Abhinay belongs to the youngsters who love maintaining their own music group with drums, guitars supporting the Western music and are tempted to look at vulgar posters. They indulge in slangs and other informal affected expressions, wearing hippy-like attires and sporting tattoos etc.

What is common between these two types is that they love, enjoy and appreciate music. Still there exists another world, the world of fashion, of boutiques, upholding high professionalism with consumerist approach. Mrs. Kapoor with the boutique reigns supreme in this world unscrupulously befooling, shallow fashionable ladies like Mrs. Screwwalla who is introduced as "a large lady in an outlandish costume, two sizes small for her". Mrs. Kapoor is the Empress of the world of fashion in "Go Go earrings, her hair piled up on top held by a chop stick. She wears chunky jewellery with stones and beads." She does not even hesitate to trap her fashion-crazy client Mrs. Screwwalla by asking her daughter for her comment when the customer tries a new fashionable dress. Though there is an apparent contrast with the world of Swarnalatha, Mr. Shastri, the villagers, the old woman, still this third world has justified the relevance of its existence. At times Mrs. Kapoor's acting clearly reveals malapropistic overtones by way of her strange sense of fashion and affected accent. Still this world is wholeheartedly accommodated with the other two worlds because Mrs. Kapoor has agreed to accommodate the youngsters preparing for the music group to practise in her boutique's storeroom.

It's another planned move on the part of the playwright to link this world with music when Balaji the owner of music store drops in Mrs. Kapoor's boutique to carry on with practice as a member of the music group. He is flabbergasted at the utter sales womanishly welcome given by the owner of the boutique. Mrs. Kapoor makes the situation messy as she behaves professionally deeming him to be a handsome young customer. The confusion is clear only when Mrs. Kapoor points him towards the storeroom. The entire music crew greet, meet and enjoy practising, keeping the tunes and beats. Its a world that thinks Goa to be the home of trance, adores seventies Hippie Hare Rama stuff, cutting jokes about their names being changed as Balaji becomes Bals while Priyanka is relegated to Pinkie and cool is affectedly articulated as 'kewl'. Munna, who cannot control himself from touching the female mannequins exposes his eroticism and is laughed at. *Pratibimb* starts its rehearsing for the final performance. Pinkie talks about some good music while Abhinay expects some variations to be tried. Everyone is assigned one's section and is supposed to maintain a cool attitude. The rehearsal begins....

"Abhinay plays the first section on his keyboard. Abhinay assigns the sections to Munna and a beat to Balaji." He insists "Pinkie, could you do a little groove after the melody? Okay, 1, 2, 3, 4...." The symphony is interrupted by 'a high pitched scream and a woman's sobbing'. Like a great maestro in trance Abhinay's rapture is broken by Mrs. Kapoor popping in and the sobbing continues. He finds it difficult to have a decent rehearsal here. His abrupt comments about Mrs. Kapoor hurt Pinkie's sense of self-prestige so much so that she shouts at him.... "You can't afford a place. That's the way my mother earns an honest living. If you don't like it, pack your stuff away." Before both of them forget to be cool by using a montage, Dattani skilfully saves their life's music from being harsh and the scratch tune they were practising is now used as a background music for this montage.

The band crew passing along the culture of coffee shops, banquet hall parties, giving their best performance, winning applauds receives a disapproving remark from the manager. Disheartened Abhinay walks as if without aim in search of some 'good music'. Against the backdrop of a park bench the lullaby sung by a boy in rags to his baby sister succeeds in winning back to Abhinay his lost mellow mood but temporarily. Friends are of no avail. He is not that cool.

His terms are out of tune with Pinkie too. Most of the time, he is haunted by the memory of his mother. One fine day half of his search is over as the postman delivers him the parcel containing a note. Swarnalatha's notes are heard from the riverside. He feels excited as he touches the texture of the violin. The picture of his mother playing the violin is screened. The camera also reveals Swarnalatha singing and Vaishnavi accompanying her. The parcelled violin proves to be a spring board to accelerate his imagination. It's through the title Pratibimb the past performance of Swarnalatha which could not be consummated is linked with music.

He decides to thank Swarnalatha for bringing him back to his roots by sending him the violin which is not only an instrument perpetuating his mother's memory but also a relic rendering him a desire to survive by continuing with music. The moment he reaches Swarnalatha with a resolution to pay tribute to his mother with music, he is mistaken. Swarnalatha's guilt ridden conscience makes her misapprehend Abhinay: "And now you have come here to blame me for your mother's death and stealing her violin." On the contrary the truth dawns when he says, "I am starting a music group and I want you to be a part of it." It's a pleasant surprise for Abhinay when she starts guiding him unknowingly the right way to play the Carnatic violin. She also teaches him the correct posture and traditional classical method to play. Music works wonders as both the protagonists are united for the pure perusal of music where the art is for arts sake. Mr. Shastri is amazed at his wife's rediscovered passion. Tremendous cathartic effect this music plays. Nobody can imagine that in end it will transcend the performers and the play as well. The modern crew of youngsters is transformed as they are happily inclined to fuse the classical Indian tradition of music to their Western type of performance. It is an amazing fusion of the two worlds of music and of the two generations as well. The tables are turned when Bals loves being addressed as Balaji and 'Priyanka' appeals much to Pinkie. They are flabbergasted when Abhinay declares "Auntie has agreed to sing for us." After having stared at him and Priyanka, Balaji and Munna take their positions with their respective roles of singing, of playing the musical instruments and of percussion on drums. Swarnalatha, the accomplished vocalist asks Abhinay from where to start and he tells "Okay, you can come in after the fifth bar." The concert begins with invocation of *Lord Ganesh* in *Raga Todi*. Disapproval by Rajeev, the director of record company, annoys Abhinay who confidently chides him. "Do you know that melody is five hundred years old? And you prefer a bubblegum jingle to it?" To Swarnalatha he says, "I cannot do the concert without you." This connects us to the past when she had challenged Abhinay's father "I will sing for your son."

In the next exterior she bumps into Abhinay's father in the temple and is offended by his comment: "Please leave him alone. Music will take him nowhere." Overcoming all such emotional jolts, she finally leaves for the banquet hall to perform the *Morning Raga*. The band players feel ecstatic but the flashback of the accident twenty years back again perturbs her. In her unconscious the 'cracked tanpura' ominously floats. The montages of Mrs. Kapoor's boutique, market place, Swarnalatha's living room make her move on finally to Abhinay's village home and she is bold enough to command Abhinay to bring his mother's violin. Abhinay's father is stunned. Swarnalatha feels the Pratibimb (reflection) of Vaishnavi in Abhinay "Let us see whether he has inherited some bhava from his mother."

Despite the momentary reconciliations the clash between the two generations and the two worlds interrupts now and when she disapproves of the noisy western music or the villagers deeming Munna to be Michael Jackson or mocking at the crew calling them city monkeys. Swarnalatha again puts forth challenge to Abhinay's father's remark "They are laughing at my son, because of you" and sarcastically she retorts "they are laughing at your son today. Tomorrow they will salute him for his talents. But then he will be Vaishnavi's son."

The next intercut shows "Swarnalatha playing the *raga*, still in a daze and the little boy finally comes into the same room to see his mother playing the violin. As if coming out of a reverie, Abhinay exclaims "That's it,", and Swarnalatha stops playing.

He continues, "That's the *raga* I want! That's what I was looking for don't you see! (To Pinkie) My mother never played it for me. She played it for her" giving vent to a sort of sibling rivalry with his mother.

Swarnalatha is hurt to the very core of her heart. Again many flashbacks rotate in her mind's eye like 'a venerable old man teaching Swarnaltha the morning raga' or Mr. Shastri abusing her for killing their son and starts feeling panicky. When Pinkie takes her for a car-ride across the bridge at a fast speed and ultimately succeeds in making Swarnalatha overcome her panic that she was not the cursed one to cause the accident leading to Vaishnavi's and Mathav's death. Pinkie tells her that it was her father who was responsible for the accident and the consecutive deaths. It dawns on Swarnalatha like the reservation of the truth. "It does not matter whose fault it was the truth is that your mother is gone and so is my son. Can any force being them back to him? Can any force bring back her father?" Listening to it Abhinay looks at her fighting his tears. Swarnalatha blessing him and Pinkie as well and finally the contents of the card sent by Abhinay with a mother and child bring in a sort of *anagnorisis* to Swarnalatha. The card reads like: "You are wrong. There are forces that can bring back your son and my mother to us. I hope one day I can help you understand how proud your son be if you sang for him. I don't know how to make you see that but I will keep trying." Being convinced to honour the invitation through Mr. Shastri she feels elated and makes up her mind to pay a tribute to her dead son Madhav and friend Vaishnavi.

Mr. Shastri and Swarnalatha are shown crossing the same bridge. She is joyous for what she thought of like an ill-omen becomes a source of pure joy. Reaching the auditorium and finally the stage, after undergoing many dilemmas of to sing or not to sing Pinkie's words: "Now it's your chance...the first number we play is called *Morning Raga*. It is the Raga you wanted to sing. The one you taught me." The music that emanates from Swarnalatha's heart is spiritually elevating. She is shown slowly walking to the mike and then begins *Sindhu Bhairvi* going into its intricate patterns. She could perform the most difficult raga the dream comes true, wish fulfillment, her real master-piece.

Even after a lapse of twenty-years, she walks along the path of music for the sake of her son whom she sees alive in form of Abhinay. She says, "I will sing this song for you my son who, like my music has returned after a very long journey. Abhinay, I sing this raga for you my son." It's a real tribute to the deaths in past and to music as well.

She performs her masterpiece, Abhinay's search finds its destination and Pinkie's sense of guilt translates into ecstasy. Swarnalatha's gradual shift from *Raga Todi* which is to be sung during night to *Sindhu Bhairavi* a Raga meant for morning is the journey from darkness to light, from dark clouds of gloom to the warm sunshine of morning and from death to life. It is truly the *Morning Raga* of life's music. It's here we find all three Swarnalatha, Abhinay and Pinkie rewarded by the law of divine compensation. What they lost about twenty years ago has been showered being infinitely multiplied unto them by the sublime power of music. The power of the music that the play portrays is, to borrow the oft-quoted lines "Neither harsh nor grating but of immense power to chasten and subdue." Its feel is similar to what Milton felt when he writes: "Calm of mind all passions spent."

Work Cited

Dattani, Mahesh. *Complete Plays: Volume Two, Screen, Stage and Radio Plays.* New York: Penguin Books, 2005. Print.

14

Stigma, Ostracism and Reconstruction of Composite Self-Identity in *Ek Alag Mausam*

Usha Jain

Dattani is a nonconformist iconoclast. With his intrepid experimental theatrical style he dares to trudge the most obscure cerebral region of human psyche and leaves enduring impression. As a sensitive human being he candidly opines and takes a stand on the contradictory socio-politico-psychological issues intimidating the modern urbanized Indian society. The maverick playwright, with his choice of theme, in the play, *Ek Alag Mausam*, again proves his ingenuity in treating an intricate social issue with psychological nuance. The title itself is suggestive of the off-beat theme which Dattani intends to handle with all somberness and conviction. Indubitably he operates as an investigator elucidating a social problem. The play was translated into a film with the same name by producer, director K.P. Sasi, released in 2005.

Despite the obvious message, it does not disintegrate into an easy edifying play but explores the extreme possibilities of human resilience even when the invisible claws of death are gripping almost every character of the play. AIDS is no corny ailment. Death is inevitable but the social stigma associated with the disease kills the patient even before the disease could devour him. The angst of humiliation rips the soul, tortures the psyche and deflates the self-esteem of the patient. Aparna is one such character who carries deep wounds of physical and emotional hurt to Jeevanjyoti—a place which tries to illumine the gloomy lives of the AIDS patient by infusing its inhabitants with the hope to live life to the lees.

The death is all pervasive in ironically named Jeevan Jyoti. It hangs heavy as George puts it, "Death is not news here. Life is" (504). In fact the iconic statement of Jeevan Jyoti, "I am alive this moment, this day" (436) conspicuously intensifies the absence of life force. Dr. Machado's devotion to the AIDS patients is singularly exceptional. He indeed is the mouthpiece of the dramatist. He honestly works hard to invigorate the dying. His ideology imbibed in his speech is an inspiration to all those who are dying before their actual death.

> You are not alone in this world. There are hundreds of thousands of people like you suffering in silence. Why? Because they all think that they are going to die. Of course they are going to die. We will all die one-day. Who is to say when? Then why this fear of dying? What is important is that we are alive today. We are alive right now.
>
> I am not HIV positive but I am also dying. But do I think about my death all the bloody time? ...No I think of each moment that I have. Each month. Each season that I have. So why don't you. You all have these moments, months, seasons.... (486)

Dattani's observation of human behaviour is impeccable. Dattani employs the flashback technique to explore the life of the leading lady Aparna. The news of being HIV positive comes as an alarm to pregnant Aparna. Overwhelmed Aparna refuses to believe it. Distressed and confused she reiterates in vain. "It just can't be!... I haven't had a sexual relationship with anyone but my husband, I haven't had any blood transfusions, I always make sure the doctor uses a disposable syringe..." (479). Further the infidelity and apathy of her husband and doctor's refusal to admit her in the nursing home shatter her completely, "we are refusing to admit you on the grounds that it will upset our nurses and other patients..." (479). When Aparna insists on retaining her pregnancy, Dr. Sanyal advises her "Don't be a fool.... No proper nursing home is going to touch you. And either your baby or you will die soon" (480).

Divorced, psychologically wounded and infected with HIV positive, Aparna needs lot of courage and power to endure the pain and ignominy. When she approaches Dr. Machado, she has neither hope nor faith in love and life, yet defiant she refuses to be counseled by the doctor, "I didn't come here to be counseled. Doctor do you need my services over here or don't you?" (490). Her depressive mental state is obvious. The life has suddenly become an empty shell, as if a gust of wind has sucked everything out of her. She ceases to find meaning in life; she confesses that she can never be happy again, "I want to make children happy. They can be happy, not I..." (498). The disease is like a death sentence to Aparna. The infidelity of her husband, the forced abortion due to the disease and the disease itself break her to the core.

Ostracism, rejection and discrimination are obviously observable facts associated with the disease. Dattani explicitly articulates the bitter, insensitive socio-psychological demeanor to HIV positive patients through his characters. Aparna is no exception. Mother's warning to Aparna speaks volume about societal attitude, "I am here for you but be careful of the world. Don't let anyone know of your illness..." (500). George's candid statement further shocks Aparna, "Who do you think takes the bodies for the cremation...? The municipality van won't even enter the compound.... So be careful if you come here often enough people will think you have Aids also" (497).

Social exclusion of Aids patients is a common global phenomenon. Dattani's insightful treatment of the intense issue reveals the brutal, unsympathetic familial and social mindset. He seems to be brooding over the frail familial relationships when it comes to a disease like Aids. George is actually thrown out of his house and village by his parents and villagers for no fault of his own. He got the disease through blood transfusion but the ignorance and stigma allied with the disease estrange him both physically and emotionally from his family. George's father refuses to accompany him and bluntly ask him to leave the village, "You may live for another seven years. But you have killed us before we have entered our graves. What face do we have left in this village? Don't come back. Leave. Go George! (making a gesture as if to a beggar) Go!" (537).

Wrecked, alienated and hurt George finds solace in Jeevan Jyoti, a rehabilitation center for Aids patients. His commitment to make children happy at Jeevan Jyoti is an expression of his gratitude to them to make his life worth living. He says to them, "You are the only ones I love" (538).

It is in the process of building the lost self-esteem and composite self-identity, Aparna too arrives at Jeevan Jyoti. The gossamer web of skepticism gradually clears up as she begins to work with children. It is actually George who teaches her the philosophy of life "Is it too much to hope for that the last few days they have that they learn to laugh, to think of their life. To seize the moment as doctor keeps saying?" (505). Vivacious George is undoubtedly a super hero of all the children at Jeevan Jyoti. Dying children find his philosophy fascinating: "Imagine that God is playing football. And the sun is his ball. When he kicks the ball, it is sunrise. The ball goes high in the air. That is noon. When it lands in the goal, it is sunset. God always scores a goal.... One kick of the ball and we get a whole day" (523). For George what matters is the day in his hand. For him it is life that matters and not the sunset or death. Death is inevitable. George's passion for life is infectious. His love for life is unsurpassed even if living includes lot of suffering. Children find meaning in his philosophy.

Without losing his focus on the central theme of Aids, Dattani deftly weaves an arresting, impressive and intense love story to the key design of the plot. His treatment of love takes the story to the sublime plane. His scattered philosophical thoughts on the grave issues like love, death, destiny and fate are insightful and prod the higher realm of consciousness.

The plot gets momentum as the character of Aparna grows through various experiences of life. She has witnessed suffering, death, infidelity and human limitations. It is George who helps her to come out of her narrow ego-centricities to the deeper understanding of life and archetypal awareness of cosmic consciousness. With this also comes the mute acceptance of disease.

George's declaration of love to Aparna comes as a shower of rain on the dry landscape. But Aparna's refusal to George is in verity a denial of life. Little Paro aptly comments: "You are running away from me now...the way you ran away from George" (474).

George's instant liking for Aparna makes her more conscious of her disease, conscientious Aparna squeezes herself furthermore into her cocoon. Her life revolves round Jeevan Jyoti. She makes it clear to George, "Yes. If there is anything that has meaning to me in my life it is this place. Jeevan Jyoti. I give to it what I can and I take whatever it gives me. There are no other demands" (532). She persistently broods about disease and death. She lives in the constant shadow of both Aids and Death. "How can I forget? It is there! Written in our medical reports. Our death warrant. We can have those test done over and over again but the truth is we will one day have Aids" (532). For Aparna being alive is Death-In-Life experience, but for George every moment of life is precious. He tries to convince Aparna, "I am not talking about the time when we won't be here. I am talking about now. All this years we have left in us. We can be therefore each other" (533). George tries to make her realize the point that no disease can snatch away the beautiful moments of life. Simply she has to open up and embrace the life. She has blindfolded herself and cannot see that both love and life are waiting for her. He pleads her not to think about Aids anymore, "You have branded yourself Aids, Aids Aids! You have put a big red stamp on yourself. I thought only an uncaring and unfeeling society would do that to us. But no. We don't have to worry about society. We are doing it to ourselves! I refuse to brand myself. All I want to know is that I love you and I want to marry you" (533).

George confesses his love to Aparna but unfortunately it remains unreciprocated as Aparna lives in constant fear of death. George values Aparna's sentiments:

> I know your every mood, your every movement. I know your fear of death. I have seen you with the children. You want to be close to them; but any demands of affection and you are suddenly as distant as the stars. I can see

> the fears in your eyes and also the desperation to love something without the fear of causing it harm. Yes I know you Aparna. I think of you all the time. I want to think of ways to make you feel happy. I have never felt this way about another woman before. (533)

Although George and Aparna are two different individuals from diverse backgrounds as doctor Machado points out, "You two are travelling in different trains. Hers is travelling non-stop to the final destination and yours is stopping at all the small towns. Besides...has it occurred to you that she is travelling first class and you...(530), but George's conviction in his love remains unshakable as he says, "Can one make sense of Destiny? Why bother even trying?" (524). The disease has brought them together, as he says, "If you and I were not HIV positive I would be driving my truck and you would be in your ivory tower. And we would never have met" (545).

George could feel Aparna's love for him, "I know she loves me as much as I love her" (530) but the twin apprehensions of Aparna, i.e. the fear of death and the cause of disease in case of George deter her from accepting him. As she says,

> Come on George! You are a truck driver and you are HIV positive! Nobody needs to guess very hard how you got infected! How can I marry you knowing that you have been infected by another woman? That you have in turn infected several others. Why do you think my husband left me? Because he couldn't face me after I knew the truth. But you are more shameless than him. You dare to ask to marry you? (534)

Dattani further develops a crisis with the revelation of the fact that the lease of Jeevan Jyoti was running out by the end of the year and landlord refused to renew it without having a heavy sum for it. Aparna organizes a charity show to raise funds to save Jeevan Jyoti. Her love for Jeevan Jyoti and children is overwhelming. She says to George, "You and I won't be here for very long, but we must make sure Jeevan Jyoti lives forever" (534). To save Jeevan Jyoti is the only mission of Aparna's life.

> They have made me happy Jeevan Jyoti is the only thing that matters now. Isn't it ironic? We wanted to find ways to keep this place running to help the children. Now the children are keeping this place running with their show so that we can be happy. I hope a time will come when they don't need us at all. I will be most happy when that day arrives. (541)

Dattani has a knack for subtle blending of shock and surprise. The money raised from the charity is not enough. It rather turns out to be a socialite evening as Dr. Machado had anticipated, "All the society type will be there, pretending to help. But they will take their publicity and do little else" (543). It is actually George who sells all his trucks and godown to save Jeevan Jyoti. Aparna, when learns the fact is shocked, surprised and moved to the core. George's decision to leave Jeevan Jyoti makes Aparna realizes her feelings for him but she still doesn't stop him , "...I know you are leaving because of me...if only...we were not HIV positive. Then may be..." (545).

Prostitute Rita, while dying with Aids had left little Paro, her daughter in Aparna's custody. Little Paro could sense Aparna's yearning for the lost child. She too wants Aparna to come out of her shell and accept her as her daughter, "if for once you can think of me as your daughter, think of the pleasure I will have while you are still there. You are so silly, aunty. You did same with George" (550).

Dattani's deft handling of the climax is the point of keenest interest in the play. While taking little Paro to admit in the school Aparna decides to meet Dr. Machado, where the fact of HIV positive blood transfusion to George is revealed to her by Dr. Machado. Dattani's dramatic art reaches to unprecedented height in portrayal of Aparna's guilt consciousness and deep regret for accusing George for concubining. Aparna's realization and confession of her love for George are the most moving moments of the play. Dr. Machado aptly remarks, "why do you have to lose something to realize you want it?" he further says, "why is that we understand the value of things only when there is danger of losing them?" (555).

The play ends on an optimistic note. Dattani not only succeeds in the dramatic presentation of a taboo subject but has been able to probe the traumas and dilemmas of HIV Positive patients emphatically. His characters and situations are close to reality and are acceptable to reason. He neither condemns, judges nor praises but leaves his audience to analyze their own social and moral attitude. The message is simple and clear: every human being on this earth deserves the life of dignity.

Work Cited

Dattani, Mahesh. *Ek Alag Mausam, Collected Plays Volume Two*. New Delhi: Penguin Books, 2005. Print.

15

Hand Shake with the Split Self

Manik Sambre

The Girl Who Touched the Stars is a radio play which Mahesh Dattani wrote for BBC Radio 4 (first broadcast on 6th March 2007) was inspired by the life of Kalpana Chawla, the first Indian woman to be in the outer space who could not come back to the Earth. It becomes the tale of Bhavna Patel. Dattani described it, "While growing up, Bhavna has a dream. She wants to fly to the moon and touch the stars. Bhavna's dreams do come true—she is an astronaut and it is now 2025, and she is the first Indian woman to fly not to the moon but to Mars. But just after take-off, the spacecraft explodes and she finds herself in space in dialogue with her childhood self" (53).

The action of the play initiates with the take-off countdown of the spacecraft carrying Bhavna and her team and later on freezes on the inward voyage of Bhavna. It is absolutely different from routine "Startrek" type of science fantasies. Tracey Neale (the Senior Producer, BBC Radio Drama) wrote in the introductory note to the play, "...Radio plays have the ability to take you into a world of imagination. In radio the pictures are all in your head—and what pictures we could create with this play!..." (53).

Quest for 'self' had been a favourite of twentieth-century literature but it will be an oversimplification if we think that that is the only theme of this play. For, the moment Bhavna realizes that her dream has come true, her quest would have ended. But no, it continues. Actually the major theme is the growth of the self. Tracey Neale rightly observes that through the radio phonic conversation taking place in the middle of space "We could explore the dilemma that confronts a woman when she wants to hold on to reality and the present but finds herself drawn into the past—when she feels a need to understand why she has become the woman she is and why she was eager to reach out and be *the girl who touched the stars*" (53). The encounter of the grown up Bhavna with the young one instigates the feeling that if there were three Bhavnas instead of two that would have been a deeper and more fulfilling quest. The loop that is missing is the teenager Bhavna who has entered the world of physical maturity but is still ignorant of the wicked ways of the world, who could not completely grasp and sort out the strange behaviour of her parents who, perhaps, insisted on sealing the young Bhavna's feeling into a cell that would break only when faced by the mature Bhavna. The mixed world of childhood and youth, aspiration and its fulfillment could find a bond in the teenager Bhavna. Not that any improvement is suggested but it is only a piece of wild imagination that Dattani could have made it more dramatic and consequently more interesting. Otherwise also, there is a lot of scope for imagination as it is a radio play. So even the addition of the third facet of the same personality can be easily introduced and the theme of the quest for the growth of self could have been more consolidated and multi-dimensional.

Gender bias and racial discrimination are hackneyed themes unless they are handled by playwrights like Dattani who has augmented and ramified them in such a novel way. Polarities are indispensable to the structure of the play. Present versus past, reality versus fantasy, parents versus children, expectations versus their negation, physical entity versus psychological existence, technological advancement versus technical failure and flamboyance opposed to hypocrisy are a few to be mentioned. Bhavna has to dive into the depth of her past life to touch the stars. The play begins with the countdown of the spacecraft rocket in a joyous mood. The drowning of the lullaby by the deafening noise of the rocket taking off symbolises the roaring leap of the childhood of a small girl into the space of complete freedom from physical bondage.

After the take off the mood changes to bizarre as talking to the media on the earth Bhavna says "I need to use the loo" (57). With the philosophic statement on dream the past of Bhavna starts peeping out "I thank God that being a woman or an Indian has nothing to do with my journey..." (58) directly expresses freedom from gender bias and racial discrimination. After the explosion the present Bhavna encounters her young counterpart and herein starts real fantasy. The young Bhavna exists in 2006 with her dreams of spaceships and space travel while Bhavna is in 2025 actually propelled off in the space in the rocket to be blown to pieces as a result of the malfunctioning of the system or a fault in the technical implementation of the science of the rocketry. So Bhavna tells the young Bhavna: "...That is the real moment and we are inside my head right now" (60). The childhood dream of young Bhavna to walk on the moon is superseded by Bhavna's mission to Mars.

The hypocrisy of Bhavna's father is brought to the forefront. Once he wanted to get rid of her but now, when she is successful and in the limelight he feels proud to be her father. Her father's interview with the journalist can be put in the category of snobbish tall talk.

There could have been no better medium than an audio device to build up the internal journey of Bhavna. For the audience, it becomes an entertaining and self-scrutinizing recreation of the scenes constructed with a chain of images presented through the audio medium. It casts a sarcastic glance on the socio-cultural structure and the resultant thinking of Indian society. It forces us to rethink about the gender discrimination that has percolated through the Indian psyche. Gender confusion is intentionally created as Bhavna calls "uncle earth" (not "mother earth") replacing "uncle moon" of the lullaby.

The most tragic part is the end of the play where in both the Bhavnas confronting the bitter truth of life are reconciled in one person but ultimately they give us the message that they are forced to be self-centred. Bhavna loves only her young counterpart and nobody else. The golden handshake between the split self has cathartic effect. One more redeeming feature is her mother's last utterance "Go, Bhavna! Set yourself free! Go where I could never go" (77) followed by a series of explosions. That, in a way, accomplishes the fusion of Bhavna's dream with the mother's urge for freedom. The play ends with the focus on the collective dream of women.

Work Cited

Dattani, Mahesh. *Brief Candle Three Plays*. New Delhi: Penguin Books India. 2010. Print. (The figures in the brackets are from this source.)

16

The Fleeting Existence: *Brief Candle*

Jyoti Taneja

"All creativity is about exploration, openness and a willingness to look at life again from a different perspective" (42-43) says Mahesh Dattani in his introduction to the play '*Brief Candle*' (2009) which sparkles emphasising the importance of the quality of our lives rather than how long we live it. The paper deals with the plight of cancer patients, their withered physiques, their fear of non-acceptance, their desires, their uncertainty, in all the impermanence of this world. The play is aptly titled '*Brief Candle*' and the flame of life flickers and dies as patients all eventually succumb to cancer by the end of the play.

In the introduction of the play Dattani says that "theatres provide a pathway to our feelings and concerns so that we can look at our life and its vicissitudes squarely in the mirror without having to wear a mask of placid existence" (3). And he asks "Why do we lead such heavy lives?" (3). The play moves with a farcical undercurrent and leaves the audience with such questions to ponder on. Yes, why do we not accept the moments as they come and live our lives to the fullest? The play is a tragi-comedy of love, of desire to live, of acceptance, of impending death. Cancer is a fatal disease typically seen as reason to sober up, but despite the inmates of the hospital fighting death and struggling to survive the play is not despairing. It is funny with a tinge of humour here and there. It also gives a powerful message of acceptance to embrace all that comes on the way, those who have laughed have made it through and the serious keep wandering with long faces.

When the play begins the audience does not know that the hotel room sequence is a 'play within a play'. Dattani has used the dramatic device very effectively, it epitomizes two important aspects of life i.e. joy and variety. We see that grief, anguish, pain, tragedy and death are inevitable in our life nevertheless there is always a leeway of reducing the pain through art.

The hospital beds and white screens and panels puzzle the audience for it opens with a scene in a hotel. The patients of the hospital stage a play about Hotel Staylonger, a comedy written by Vikas Sharma, who died of cancer at the Avedna Cancer Institute. The institute is going to celebrate founder's day. Three patients of the hospital who knew Vikas decide to enact a play written by him in his memory. The actors are the inmates of the hospital who are ill and struggling with life. The title is a perfect metaphor 'Hotel Staylonger', where the story of the play is an attempt to have an optimistic look at death by making the hospital a hotel. Dattani conveys it is more important to keep up with the quality of our lives till we live. Mahesh and Amol are stuck because of the delayed flight and have to stay in the Hotel,

> Mahesh: ...So make the most of your stay at Hotel... and Amol repeats, 'Make the most of your stay in Hotel Staylonger,' may your stay be long. (Scene 1, 10)

These characters of the play have come to Hotel Staylonger waiting for their scheduled flights, just like we all staying in this world waiting for our flight to take off. There is supposed to be no death here, but we know the cold hands of death leave none and death stands as the ultimate winner in the play as one patient after another surrenders to death. The dead writer of the play, a former patient of the hospital, makes his fellow-inmates act out their deepest wishes and brings them face to face with their true selves. The chief doctor Deepika Dave plays the hotel manager, she is allotting rooms to the passengers of a delayed flight. Deepika as a doctor strives to extend the lives of these patients and here as a manager she is managing the stay of the patients. It is made clear that like hotel guests, our time of stay in this world is limited and as we 'check in' we also have to 'check out' and there is an end time to our life here on earth, but we don't know when. Uncertainty of life is just like a flight taking off and we don't know when we are going to land.

Amol is not sure when he is going to get his flight the next day "But we don't know when we are flying tomorrow, day after or never" (Scene 1, 10).

The characters in the play await their departures, the characters of the play end up in comic situations, as they get involved in secret flirtations and complicated love affairs. Amar is presented as a sex-maniac in the play. Dattani brings up the desire to live with the longing to love regardless of any affliction. Amar, a character in Vikas's play is suffering from prostate cancer, yet is confident of satisfying a woman, his insecurity is reflected in his confidence and he says, "And once I am in her room, could you have some wine sent to the room, but don't take too long. But not if the 'Do not Disturb' sign is turned on" (Scene 1, 9).

There is a mix of emotions, hurt, anger, fear, desire, attachments the central theme explicating the mental and physical plight and pain of cancer patients. Amarinder and Shanti reveal their embodied pains. Their physical bodies are diseased and derogated which has scarred their sense of gender and identity. They question their identity. Amarinder's narrative is incarnation of the very notion of maleness which is at stake.

> Amarinder: They never told me that they will be drilling inside my body. At my core. What made me a man? Climbing a mountain, playing a game of hockey, knowing I could satisfy a woman in bed. All that was under attack with a group of needles probing at my prostrate, through the wall of my rectum. Like being sodomized with metal. (Scene 3, 23)

Similarly Shanti, suffering from breast cancer reminisces about the critical changes her body has undergone.

> Shanti: 'I lay exposed to the technicians, my breast pushed against the X-ray plate. One of them marked my lumps, treating my breasts as if it were already a piece of dead flesh.... Their job was to invade my body and take out

> tumours, and they did. But they grew and came back till they took it all out. A part of me that I had barely felt. That I had never seen fully myself. Gone. (Scene 5, 32)

The ruthless tactlessness of the medical treatment is diverted to manhood and womanhood, and the audience is pulled by the complexities of the relationship between the dead writer and the doctor. There is a continuous fluctuation and the attention of the audience wavers as to what exactly Dattani wants to convey. The young Dr. Deepika Dave is just recovering from the loss of her lover, Vikas Sharma, as the institute prepares to stage a play written by him. Issues related to life and death are reflected and the actors, the patients of the hospital, find themselves one with the characters they have chosen to portray. Shanti, is left by her husband after detection of breast cancer, she plays the role of a single woman looking for companionship. And the man she finds is the character suffering from prostate cancer who is worried about the treatment which may affect his masculinity. The plot deals with sexuality and how medical problems often lead to further taboo evoking a common theme of love in the lives of all the characters as each of them looks for reasons to fight death, to survive and live to the fullest whatever time is left with them. The play is a comedy in the true sense of the word because the characters seem to have gained more of understanding of their lives. The play addresses not just the joy of life but analyses the pain and misery of death in a new light. A few laugh at their portrayal by Vikas in his play and some struggle when they face the truth and their own demons. Each patient is fighting a battle, the long monologues of Vikas, Amol, Amarinder, and Shanti convey their deepest fears, their illness and its effect on their lives. Shanti narrates everything right from her wedding night to the hospital, her pathetic condition her husband and later on Amarinder are horrified seeing her as a lesser woman.

> Shanti: 'On my wedding night my husband put on some music and danced. He wanted me to dance with him. I wasn't prepared for that....
>
> Our maid showed me the blood stains on my brassiere. She thought I had hurt myself....

> Their job was to invade my body and take out tumours, and they did....
>
> Till they took it all out. A part of me that I had barely felt. That I had myself never seen. Gone.' (Scene 5, 31-32)

Similarly the Viagra jokes were for humour but once we know that the man had prostate cancer, the jokes become painful conveying life is a mesh of tragedy and comedy.

As the stories of the patients reveal, we understand how Dattani has used theatre to bring out catharsis, how the young doctor Deepika probes deep into the psyche of her patients, how the dead playwright Vikas puts his own understanding into the play and brings forth real pain and sorrow before the audience. The fine line between comedy and tragedy merges and the characters going through a crucial sense of loss keep themselves away from it. This is how life is to be witnessed from a distance and make the gloom, the despair, the impermanence of life more meaningful, live with affirmation and remain joyful.

Brief Candle is an emotional, touching play with a blend of humor and pathos. Thought he connect with the characters and their dilemmas leave the spectators sentimental with tears in their eyes, yet it leaves a powerful message of life, analysing the misery of death, of the grim realities of the disease stressing on the quality of life we need to spend and not on how long we live...as I said those who have laughed have got through and the serious are still wandering with long faces.

Work Cited

Dattani, Mahesh. *Brief Candle Three Plays*. Penguin Books, New Delhi, 2010. Print. (The figures given in brackets refer to this publication.)

17

Mixing Memory and Desire: Revisiting Shakuntala in *Where Did I Leave My Purdah?*

Urbashi Barat

> What is a historical fact? A spent shell? A bombed-out building? A pile of shoes? A victory parade? A long march? Once it has been suffered it maintains itself in the mind of witness or victim, and if it is to reach anyone else it is transmitted in words or on film and it becomes an image, which, with other images, constitutes a judgment.
>
> E.L. Doctorow, "False Documents"

> In order to cope with a trauma, we symbolize.
>
> Slavok Žižek, *On Belief*

Perhaps no other contemporary Indian play in English so obviously exemplifies the performativity of identity, and illustrates the perception that social reality is continually created through performance, than Mahesh Dattani's *Where Did I Leave My Purdah?* The play is a celebration of theatre; as Michael Wailing of the theatre company Border Crossings, for instance, has observed, in a comment that Dattani has reproduced on his Facebook wall: "Like Mamet's 'A Life in the Theatre', 'Where Did I Leave My Purdah?' is a thank you letter, a homage, and a hymn of praise to the theatrical life." Dattani's explanation of the implications of his title points to the importance of the theatre motif in this play: "Purdah means a partition between man and woman, and also, it's the veil of modesty which an actor has to give up very early on in life. One has to marvel at the actresses who took on the stage as a profession because there was a stigma attached that it was nothing less than prostitution. I also refer to it as the purdah of the stage" (qtd. in Ancheri). As the title *Where Did I Leave My Purdah?* itself suggests, then, Nazia has left her 'purdah' along the way; her play makes her look back, and helps her to discover where and why. Its play-within-a-play encapsulates, symbolizes and enables the performer-protagonist's moral and emotional growth.

Theatre and performance have of course been an intrinsic part of all Dattani's drama; his plays illustrate, in an extension of the concept of theatrum mundi, Richard Schechner's words, "The world...[is not] a book to be read but...a performance to participate in" (qtd. in Banerjee). In Dattani's plays they are a metaphor, a symbol, for some of the deepest, most unspeakable and unspoken truths of life. He himself has stated:

> Man has created a very complex language called theatre. A language that has the ability to redefine the natural concepts of time, space and movement. A language that goes beyond the verbal, a movement that goes beyond the physical. Through this language of theatre he has been able to see himself for who he is, what he has made of himself and what he aspires to be. ("Contemporary Indian Theatre and its Relevance")

This is particularly so in *Where Did I Leave My Purdah?* (henceforth, *Purdah*), which continually points out, through Nazia's story counterpointed with the stories of Shakuntala, the Shakuntala of myth and of Kalidasa's play and the Shaku of Nazia's, that theatre empowers both actor and audience to confront and accept these truths.

As several reviewers, like, for instance, Saumya Ancheri, have pointed out, and as Dattani himself has told Punjani, Nazia is clearly inspired by the inimitable and irrepressible Zohra Sehgal, although, obviously, this is not her story; her theatre group, The Modern Indian Theatre is, as Dattani has stated, based on the IPTA, the Naya Theatre, and Prithvi Theatre, the first two of which in particular "wanted to introduce ideas of freedom and expression into the political climate of a new country" (Ancheri). Indeed, Nazia's attempts to revive her old company with a modern retelling of the play that had once made them famous is reminiscent of the revival of the IPTA and its retelling of the story of Anarkali, making it, first, a story about 'honour killing' and then, more recently, about father-son relationships.

A feisty old stage actress, spirited enough even to reject the indignity of chemotherapy in her struggle with cancer (5) Nazia is now confined to stereotypical grandmother roles in 'mainstream' formulaic Hindi films. Then, just as she has to go, very reluctantly, for another uninspiring film shot, she has an "epiphany" (Ancheri): "This is it. There's always a time in your life that the truth strikes you"—a declaration full of dramatic irony—and goes on: "I am going back to the theatre!... My life is big. I am BIG and GENEROUS! Only the theatre deserves me!" (4-5). Revisiting Shakuntala, the role and the play for which she was once famous and with which she was once identified, is an intrinsic part of her return to the stage and to that moment when "the truth strikes you"; it helps her to rediscover herself, renew her relationships, and understand the past, not only hers, but of those of nation and community, in the broadest sense of those two terms, for Abhijnana Shakuntalam is more than a youthful romance; it is ultimately a tale of the idea of India. Shakuntala and Dushyant are, it must be remembered, the parents of Sarvadamana, 'one who conquers all', Prince Bharata, after whom India is named:

> Their characters are in one way or the other responsible for the other world, the everyday world outside the theater [sic]. Duşyanta and Śakuntala are the father and the mother of the ancestor of the Indian nation, Bharata. (Gerow 45-46)

The favourite of Orientalists like Sir William Jones, it has been the most well-known Indian play for the West for over two centuries, and is staged even today. (For instance, Dr. Grant Shen of the National University of Singapore directed a production in 2012.) W.J. Johnson calls it "the paradigmatic Sanskrit play...which has provided a benchmark for all classical

Indian literature." Not only that: it is "the validating aesthetic creation of a civilization, a play whose form and content unite to 'express persistent cultural verities'" (x). Revisiting Shakuntala, then, is to interrogate these social and cultural "verities" and their relevance today.

India today is a nation born of religious and social strife, of partition killings and 'gang-rape', of displays of murderous patriarchal power masquerading as the desire for freedom and identity. Nazia has lived through it all: as a young theatre artist playing the role of Shakuntala in Lahore in 1948; she has even killed the man who was trying to murder the Hindu Suhel, her Dushyant in the play and her beloved in real life. Fleeing to India with Suhel and her older sister, Zarine, for the sake of her theatre and her love, she has seen Zarine murdered by her co-religionists because she had not worn a burqa—the 'purdah' that would have saved her; Zarine had sworn on the Koran to look after her younger sister and had given her her own burqa to protect her. She has had to identify Zarine's body amid a pile of corpses, recognizing her only because of the 'ring of recollection' (in an ironic reference to Kalidasa) she had worn; she had covered her sister with that burqa for a kafan, and she has never worn a veil since then (*Purdah* 51). The horrors she has to go through do not end there. Once in India the burqa that had protected her in Pakistan proves to be her undoing: she is raped by several men only because her 'purdah' had identified her as a Muslim, and is left pregnant as a result. And the same Suhel for whom she had killed a man and left her home in Lahore does nothing, can do nothing, to save her, then and now. She rejects his pity and his attempts to help her:

> I don't need your pity! It is so easy to put someone down by pitying them...and I need you to help me? So you can take control over my life. Oh there are too many women in dance and theatre who have succumbed to those tactics. Too many who allow men to ruin their lives. But I am not one of them. (29)

She feels he has repudiated her, just like Shakuntala had been by Dushyant, whose role Suhel continues to play, because the child in her womb was not his. In the end Suhel leaves her, for his presence in her life and in the play only sharpens her wounds and does not allow her to "move on" from the trauma of the past:

> You want to forget the past? I am your past. I was hoping we would have a future together which could somehow heal both of us...[sic] I hope the company will give you the solace you seek. (31)

But that does not happen. The theatre company disintegrates and Nazia is reduced to acting in films that give her no satisfaction. She raises her child alone, like Shakuntala, but unlike Shakuntala has not acknowledged the child as her own, preferring to let it be known that Ruby is the dead Zarine's daughter. Ruby has grown up hating Nazia, believing she had not allowed Zarine the credit of being the Shakuntala of the Modern Indian Theatre, believing, even, in fact, that she had killed Zarine in her desire for Shakuntala's role (46). Now, when Nazia finds she has no sponsors for her version of Kalidasa's play—they all want the old, safe story—Ruby decides to help on condition that she acknowledges Zarine and Suhel, whom she believes to be her father; she also tries to shock Nazia into admitting the truth about her parents, jogging her memory, she says with sarcasm, with a "memento" from the past, just like Dushyant had needed one (39). This is no inanimate ring, however, but her own daughter, Nikhat, who looks just like the young Nazia, an aspiring actor whom Nazia has never seen before, holding a poster of Shakuntala from the past. Just as Dushyant realizes after the ring had been found: "After seeing this ring, all those memories tumble through my mind like a waterfall without any banks. They pound at my mind, like the look in her eyes when I rejected her, inflicting wounds on my soul!" (42). Nazia is compelled to tell the truth, but it is a truth very different from what Ruby and Nikhat had imagined, one that

> we don't want to acknowledge.... We will weave these tangled webs around the truth, so we can strangle it and make it disappear. We are all deceiving one another. (48)

Nazia agrees that it was Zarine who had played Shakuntala all those years back, although it was she herself on stage: "when I played the part, she always took over", because Zarine had always wanted the role and Nazia had persuaded her to flee from Lahore with her by promising it to her it, a promise she had not been able to keep. She also agrees that she had killed Zarine for the sake of the role: she had fled Lahore because she had killed a man, but also because she had loved theatre and Shakuntala, and had wanted Zarine to go with her—a decision that had caused her death. Zarine had to die for Nazia's desire to live.

Dattani once remarked in an interview with Deepa Punjani that his Thirty Days in September was "based on the triumph of the human spirit over any attempt to quell its dignity". This is even more the case with *Purdah*. Nazia's triumph lies not simply in successfully producing her new version of Shakuntala but, rather, in the way she is able to rise above the horrors of her past by doing so. She is a performer not just by profession; she is a performer in her personal life as well, repressing and repudiating memories and desires that would have devastated most other people, memories that "hide in a dark corner like a ghoul and grab at you when you are not looking. And sometimes you have to beat the shit out of the ghoul to make it crawl back into its dark corner" (24), and desires that must remain unspoken. That is why her vision of Shakuntala has to be different from Kalidasa's. Her Shakuntala is Shaku and King Dushyant Dash. Shaku is not the "virtuous female (satī), the propriety of whose actions is founded ultimately on the redemption of the hero's actions", as Kalidasa's Shakuntala is (Gerow 49), not "this whiny little creature whose entire future depends on whether her husband can remember having slept with her or not" (38), but a girl who accepts her single motherhood and gets on with life, a person who knows "what it feels like when you recognize someone. Truly recognize a person. What does it mean to you today? That's what Shaku is about" (10). Together, Shakuntala's and Nazia's stories develop into an image of the trauma of individuals and the burden of history, an image through which catharsis occurs and equanimity and reconciliation are achieved. Nazia's story unfolds through her attempts to produce her own version of Shakuntala's story, one which she intends would represent the truths of contemporary India. Until all these experiences from her past are recalled and represented, in images that form what

Doctorow calls "false documents", her ghosts cannot be laid and a new Sarvadamana be born, an India in which, as in post-apartheid South Africa, truth and reconciliation can establish a new and harmonious society. Thus theatre and performance become in *Purdah* a mode by which society can reflect and define itself by dramatizing its collective myths and history, and eventually transform both itself and the individuals who are involved in this performance (to paraphrase John MacAloon's description of performance in Rite, Drama, Festival, Spectacle).

After her play is performed and Shakuntala revisited Nazia finds she can believe that Suhel had not rejected her because she was pregnant with a child conceived from rape, that he had left her because he felt that his presence in her life would only make her memories of wounds fester, and can acknowledge with affection the role he had played in her life: "This play is dedicated to Suhel. The finest artist I ever met. And the most loving husband a woman can possibly have" (55). She can also recall Zarine without guilt or grief, and accept that her sister would have made a far better Shakuntala than she ever was, not so much because of her "histrionic" abilities but because she was more like Kalidasa's heroine than Nazia: "I don't think I was right for the part. It belonged to my sister. A very kind, beautiful, generous, evolved soul. Like Shakuntala. Something I can never be in this lifetime" (55). At last she can "move on", get on with life, which for her is symbolized in drama:

> Dance away! And act like life is one big performance with a standing ovation waiting at the end of it! Spin me around! Oh this wheelchair is too small for all the life's left in me. (55)

It is through theatre, then, that she finds her core, her identity, and reconciliation and acceptance.

So do the other characters. In the process of staging the play Ruby, Nazia's daughter, discovers the truth of her identity, and understands why Nazia had never been able to show her any love, although, as Suhel has just told her before he died, she did care very much. Her anguish and bitterness at Nazia's apparent rejection had spilled over into her relationship with her own daughter, Nikhat: a series of rejections that are foreshadowed by those in Shakuntala, notably, Shakuntala's own abandonment by Menaka, her mother; her and her son's reputation by Dushyant; and the king's rejection of his other wives. When old memories are released and old desires remembered and rekindled harmony can be restored, between Nazia and Ruby, between Ruby and Nikhat, between Nazia and Suhel, between the past and the present. Even Vinay, the assistant director of the film in which Nazia had an undistinguished grandmother's role, fulfills his desire of becoming an actor when Nazia gives him the lead role of Dushyant in her play, and in the process realizes the truth of his own sexuality that he had so far refused to accept. "Theatre", he tells the audience at the end of a performance of Shaku, "is about recognizing who you are" (54). Revisiting Shakuntala, then, is to revive memories and awaken desires. In and through Nazia's revisiting of Kalidasa's play, old ghosts are laid to rest, and new vistas open.

For the first time in his dramatic oeuvre Dattani uses myth as themise-en-abyme. One of the most obvious effects of myth in drama is, of course, that it cuts off the moorings of the play to a particular time and space. Shakuntala's story in the Mahabharata and in Kalidasa becomes a forerunner to Nazia's apparently very different one; it resonates throughout history and geography as a symbol of both trauma and reconciliation. This is reinforced by the constant switches in time and space, which Dattani effects through his favourite split-stage technique, which continually blends past and present, Lahore and Mumbai, together seamlessly; indeed, the stage directions explicitly state, "It is important that the scenes play one into the other with no blackouts." Moreover, Dattani requires his actors to play multiple parts, which further ensures the smooth and continuous overlapping of all the stories. The actress who plays Ruby, Nazia's daughter who has grown up believing she is Nazia's niece and Zarine's daughter, also plays Zarine, and as Zarine plays Anusuya, Shakuntala's friend. Nikhat, Ruby's daughter, is the young Nazia; as Nazia she plays the role of Shakuntala in their theatre company. Vinay is Suhel from Nazia's past, who had played Dushyant in the old Shakuntala; he now plays Dash in Shaku.

On the surface there seems to be little if anything in common between Kalidasa's demure forest-maiden Shakuntala, the traditional epitome of the ideals of Indian womanhood—young, innocent, beautiful, obedient, who accepts her repudiation with sorrow and dignity, and waits patiently to be reunited with her husband,—and the elderly Nazia, whose ebullience, uninhibited tongue and robust individualism embraces the present and rejects the past. Reviewers have either found that "the tragic affinity with Shakuntala" is "more or less hidden" (Prajna Desai) or, like Deepa Mohan and Kritika Pramod Kulshreshta, believe that it is Dushyant's forgetting of Shakuntala that is paralleled by the real-life Nazia herself "opt[ing] to forget her own traditions and family in Lahore" (Mohan). But the fact is that Nazia has forgotten nothing; she cannot forget, no matter how hard she tries. As Homi Bhabha has observed, in another context, memory, remembering, is really a "re-mamboing"; it is "never a quiet act of introspection or retrospection. It is a painful re-membering, a putting together of the dismembered to make sense of the trauma of the present" (63). Nazia might try to block (the Lacanian Verdrängung) or ban (Lacan's Verwerfung) these memories, memories of destroyed hopes and desires, but where her Verdrängung disguises and pushes them back, without being able ever to expel them, her Verwerfung deceives her and causes hostility, bitterness and grief in her relationships, as seen in her equations with Suhel and Ruby. Producing Shaku is almost like a psychoanalytical process of releasing these pent-up memories and finding through this release an understanding and acceptance of what happened.

Why the Shakuntala story that forms the point of reference in *Purdah* is Kalidasa's adaptation of the myth and not the original epic version may be explained, first, by the obvious fact, of course, that it is already a play, and therefore ready to be performed. A story of star-crossed young lovers who finally reunite and live happily ever after, its idyllic forest setting and its lyrical descriptions of nature have made it popular through the ages. It is only natural that the youthful members of Nazia's theatre group more than sixty years ago in Lahore should be attracted to its high romance and happy ending and make it "the grandest performance of our repertoire" (6).

But there is something more. What makes Kalidasa's version different from the original Mahabharata one is particularly significant for the purposes of this paper: he mixes memory into an old story of desire through the invention of Durvasa's curse. (Kalidasa makes other significant changes, too, but they are not pertinent to the subject of this paper.) In the Mahabharata the king repudiates Shakuntala and his young son, pretending he has no memory of their marriage because he is embarrassed by his desire that had led to a secret and possibly unacceptable marriage; it is only when the heavens intervene that Dushyant repents and recalls Shakuntala. In Kalidasa, too, desire is all-important. His play is not a simple tale of romantic love: Dushyant has many other wives, whom he has apparently wooed as ardently but whose attractions he easily forgets when he sees Shakuntala. His hunting of the deer itself is of a piece with his hunting of Shakuntala and of his other queens: a king who is always mindful of his royal duties, he is also the aggressive hunter who pursues his prey relentlessly, be it woman or nature. In both the Mahabharata and Kalidasa Shakuntala and Dushyant are overcome by desire and marry in haste, without Kanva's approval or presence; but in Kalidasa, they are also victims of memory. Shakuntala is so lost in her memories of her recently wed husband that she forgets her duties towards the sage, whose curse makes Dushyant lose his. Shakuntala's memories and forgetfulness together bring about her husband's loss of memory and loss of desire. Dushyant regains his memory only when the "ring of recollection" is found. By bringing the curse into the story, then, Kalidasa absolves Dushyant of guilt, and the audience is reassured that because Shakuntala had fallen in love with someone who was truly worthy of her she would surely be reunited with him. The ending, therefore, is thoroughly satisfactory, and upholds the traditional, albeit patriarchal, social and moral values that India has generally accepted. No wonder, then, that the young actress auditioning for the part of Nazia's Shaku excuses her failure to match up to Nazia's expectations by saying: "Maybe its [sic] the modern version I can't understand. But the original one—it makes sense.... A woman does want her child to have a father. She does forgive the man for his shortcomings" (42-43). Ultimately, Nazia too learns to forgive the man and reconcile with the past. This is what Zarine had urged her to do in her dreams: "Now play the part. Forgive Dushyant. He is after all a man. They forget...[sic]" (32). Staging Kalidasa's play had sharpened old wounds and let them fester within her. But after her version is performed, her memories are released, purged of bitterness. The play ends the young Nazia whirling around "like a kathak dancer" and the elderly Nazia of today whirling round in her wheelchair at the same time, calling out, "Thank you, Zarine! I will see you in Paradise!" (55).

As is well known, memory is the leitmotif of all Kalidasa's plays. Barbara Stoler Miller calls his drama "theatre of memory". Her introduction to Patanjali's Yoga elaborates upon the importance of memory in Sanskrit aesthetics and discusses the use of memory in this play in particular, concluding: "Memory, then, is not a discursive recollection of past events but rather an intuitive insight into the past that transcends personal experience into the imaginative.... Liberation of the spirit is possible only when subconscious subliminal impressions [that is, memory] are consumed..." (16-17). This, as has been stressed throughout this paper, is what happens in *Purdah* too. Dattani himself says that he chose Shakuntala for Nazia because both are 'memory plays':

> "Performing artists after a certain age have so many vivid memories because they've led such rich lives," Dattani said. They continue to live in the present but somewhere those memories also need to be put to rest.... Shakuntala is really about a selective kind of memory—there are some things that are maybe too painful or convenient to forget—and it is the recognition of symbols that represent that memory [that cause] those memories to come flooding in. (Ancheri)

All Dattani's plays, too, can be called 'memory plays'; they all turn upon banked down and repudiated memories that cause immense suffering in the present. The secrets of the past bear heavily on the present and have to be released for the restoration of stability and harmony.

The point is that there are some memories that are so painful, some desires that are so disturbing, that they can be represented only by image and symbol that are beyond direct representation. As Cathy Caruth explains in Unclaimed Experience; Trauma, Narrative and History, past trauma, past horrors, cannot be perceived when they occur nor retold later unless through an 'objective correlative', as it were. In the words of Slavoj Zizek, "what cannot be said must be shown." Every attempt to "reproduce the facts" in a documentary way neutralizes the traumatic impact of the events described—or as Lacan...put it: truth has the structure of a fiction...when truth is too traumatic to be confronted directly, it can only be accepted in the guise of a fiction.

Shakuntala the role and *Shakuntala* the play, Kalidasa's and Nazia's, are thus the objective correlative for Nazia's trauma. Trauma, in Freudian terms, is "a wound inflicted not upon the body but upon the mind", so that "knowing and not knowing are entangled in the language of trauma" (1, 4). This wound brings about an "internal psychic splitting" of the self, into one who experiences and one who survives. Nazia has incorporated her trauma but she has not been able to acknowledge it:

> There can be no thought of speaking to someone else about our grief under these circumstances. The words that cannot be uttered, the scenes that cannot be recalled, the tears that cannot be shed—everything will be swallowed along with the trauma that led to the loss. Swallowed and preserved. (Abraham and Torok 100, 130)

Nazia's split self is visualized in the two images of Shakuntala, Kalidasa's and her own, and it is only when her version of the play, in which Shakuntala is now Shaku, no more a victim but a triumphant survivor, is performed, that the incorporated trauma, which Abraham and Torok call antimetaphor, blocking access to acknowledgement and recovery, finds release. Nazia's split selves are reunited.

Nazia's desire for a new Shakuntala who will symbolize her own desires, aspirations and achievements and the realities of the woman's condition thus mirrors Kalidasa's desire for a new

Shakuntala who could symbolize his vision of life, in which the conflict between desire and duty is made evident through the workings of memory and ends with their reconciliation through their son, who as a future chakravartin and householder would combine desire and duty within himself (Gerow 59, Johnson xviii-xix). The mirror-image implicit in the metaphor that André Gide used for the play-within-a-play, mise-en-abyme, is an indication of the self-reflexivity of the device: "a 'mise en abyme' is any internal mirror that reflects the whole of the narrative by simple, repeated or 'specious' (or paradoxical duplication)" (Dällenbach 36). Nazia's story is a distorted-mirror-image of Shakuntala's trauma, her pain, her rejection, her struggle to discover herself, a 'specious' or 'paradoxical duplication', as Dällenbach has it. It is only when she is able to find a symbol for her trauma, in Shakuntala, that she finds forgiveness and acceptance.

Works Cited

Abraham, Nicolas and Maria Torok. *The Shell and the Kernel*. I. Trans. Nicholas Rand. Chicago: Univ. of Chicago P, 1994. Print.

Ancheri, Saumya. Rev. of *Purdah* on Nov. 23, 2012. http://www.timeoutmumbai.net/theatre/reviews/where-did-i-leave-my-purdah. Web.

Banerjee, Samipendra. "Ravaged Bodies, Embodied Performances: Performativity in Dattani's Brief Candle." *Rupkatha Journal of Interdisciplinary Studies in Humanities*. http://rupkatha.com/dattani-brief-candle/. Web.

Bhabha, Homi J. *The Location of Culture*. London: Routledge, 1994. Print.

Caruth, Cathy. *Unclaimed Experience: Trauma, Narrative and History*. Baltimore: The Johns Hopkins Univ. P, 1996. Print.

Dällenbach, Lucien. *The Mirror in the Text*. Trans. Jeremy Whitely. Chicago: Univ. of Chicago P, 1989. Print.

Dattani, Mahesh. "Contemporary Indian Theatre and Its Relevance." *The Journal of Indian Writing in English* Vol. 30, No. 1 (2002): 1-4. Print.

——. *Where Did I Leave My Purdah?* Unpub. draft. Commissioned by Prime Time Theatre Company 2012. (The figures in bracket pertaining to *Purdah* are from this source.)

Desai, Prajna. Rev of *Purdah*. http://www.mumbaitheatreguide.com/dramas/reviews/14-english-play-review-where-did-i-leave-my-purdah.asp. Web.

Doctorow, E.K. "False Documents" qtd. in Eric Heyne, "Toward a Theory of Literary Nonfiction". *Modern Fiction Studies*, Vol. 33, no. 3, Autumn 1987. 479-89. Print.

Freud, Sigmund. *Beyond the Pleasure Principle*. Trans. James Strachey. NY: Norton, 1989. Print.

Gerow, Edwin. "Sanskrit Dramatic Theory and Kālidāsa's Plays". In Miller, *The Plays of Kālidāsa*. 42-62. Print.

Johnson, W.J. Introduction. *Kālidāsa: The Recognition of Śakuntala*. Trans. W.J. Johnson. Oxford World's Classics. Oxford: Oxford Univ. P, 2001. x-xxix. Print.

Kalidasa. *Śakuntalā and the Ring of Recollection*. Trans. Barbara Stoler Miller. In Miller, *The Plays of Kālidāsa*. 85-176. Print.

Kulshreshta, Kritika Pramod. Rev of *Purdah*. *Youth ki Awaz: Mouthpiece for the Youth*. October 13, 2012. http://www.youthkiawaaz.com/2012/10/play-review-where-did-i-leave-my-purdah/. Web.

MacAloon, John J., ed. *Rite, Drama, Festival, Spectacle: Rehearsals Toward a Theory of Cultural Performance*. Philadelphia: Institute for the Study of Human Issues, 1984. Print.

Miller, Barbara Stoler, ed. *The Plays of Kālidāsa: Theater of Memory*. Delhi: Motilal Banarsidass, 1999. Print.

———. Introduction. *Yoga: Discipline of Freedom: The Yoga Sutra Attributed to Patañjali*. Berkeley: Univ. of California P, 1996. 1-26. Print.

Mohan, Deepa. Rev. of *Purdah*. 18 Dec. 2012. *Citizen Matters*. http://bangalore.citizenmatters.in/blogs/deepa-s-jottings/blog_posts/4742-where-did. Web.

Punjani, Deepa. Interview with Mahesh Dattani for THE BIG FAT CITY. http://www.mumbaitheatreguide.com/dramas/interviews/17-mahesh-dattani-interview.asp. Web.

Žižek, Slavoj. *On Belief*. London: Routledge, 2001. Print.

———. "Slavoj Žižek: What Cannot Be Said Must Be Shown". In *Less Than Nothing: Hegel and the Shadow of Dialectical Materialism*. http://simongros0.wordpress.com/2013/08/07/slavoj-zizel-what-cannot-be-said-must-be-shown/. Web

18

Silence Revealed: Articulating the Inarticulate in *Where Did I Leave My Purdah?*

Shachi Sood

Recently, much has been written by many writers about the nature of violence during and after the Partition which constitutes the thematic corpus of Partition Literature. The exceptionally thought-provoking work *Where Did I Leave My Purdah?* (2012) by Mahesh Dattani deals with the theme of partition in a ground-breaking manner. The violence that was unleashed during partition was massive and the worst sufferers were the women and children especially women of all communities were at the receiving end. Dattani perceives that the males of both the communities took revenge by committing violence on the womenfolk of the opposite community. Rather than portraying women as feeble and pitiable creatures the dramatist highlights his women protagonist as potent, vocal and ingenious.

Partition as an event of shattering corollary, retains its pre-eminence even today, despite two wars on the borders and wave after wave of communal violence. At partition, women became sites of contestation for the men of different religious communities and women's bodies bore the brunt of violence and sexual assaults. However, the physical markings and memories carried by thousands of women allow them to fulfill a more subversive role.

Within patriarchal structures, women are often believed to be the embodiment of the honour of the whole community to which they belong. Accordingly, in times of ethnic, religious or other violent conflict, they become the major targets as attacking a woman's body signifies an assault on the family and the community. The play is written against the historical background of the Indian Freedom Movement and the partition of India is an important aspect interwoven with the tormenting narrative of man-woman relationship. Commenting on the gendered and sexed female body that bears the burden of excessive symbolization, critic Graeber writes, "Victory is celebrated on a woman's body, and vengeance is taken on a woman's body" (11).

Dattani presents the gendered nature of partition with a fresh perspective by moving beyond the bitter reality of women destitution and mass widowhood and highlighting the emergence of women of forthright views and progressive outlook in his partition plays. In *Where Did I Leave My Purdah?,* Dattani conveys his vision through his women protagonist who display commendable toughness despite confronting the chaos of partition. The play highlights Dattani's attempt to explore how the violence enacted on women exists at the juncture of women as symbols of communities and as sexed individuals. As Jasodhara Bagchi and Subhoranjan Dasgupta argue, 'the easiest way to assail a community is to defile the sexual purity of its women' (4).

The episodes of violence against women during communal riots bring to the surface the notion that a woman's body is an opportunity for revenge during the partition. As a symbol of the macro community or state and nation, women's dishonor was linked to the nation, race and country. Because of this concept in the community, men did not consider women as human beings who deserve respect as well; women were just a symbol and tools for more important things including the nation or state. Commenting on the use of women bodies as the preferred sites for the hieroglyphics of power during partition, Menon and Bhasin aptly aver:

> The most predictable form of violence experienced by women, as women, is when the women of one community

> are sexually assaulted by the men of the other, in an overt assertion of their identity and a simultaneous humiliation of the other by "dishonouring" their women. (41)

The humiliation and dishonour which women were subjected to during partition has been depicted in the life of an octogenarian former Muslim film star Nazia Sahiba who is forced to recollect her glorious days of historical theatre in the pre-partition days. However, with her determination and courage she revives her faded theatre in 1950s despite her husband's betrayal and society's denial of her talent. The play is a poignant depiction of a series of tribulations which Nazia faces during partition be it the trauma of being gang raped by men of other community in front of her husband; giving birth to a child who is born out of this heinous act or witnessing the cold blooded killing of her sister. After experiencing the pain of all these incidents Nazia's character undergoes a complete transformation which is not that of lamenting at the past but looking towards the future.

Dattani alludes to the myth of Shakuntala to exhibit how Nazia revolts against the patriarchal image of women in India. Shakuntala epitomizes patriarchal subjugation of women who is beautiful and is destined to submit herself to male hegemony where she is used, abused and reduced. Nazia in her pre-partition career as a film star rejoiced at performing the role of charming and sacrificing Shakuntala. Nevertheless, her encounter with the savagery and barbarism during partition evolves her into a rebellious woman who openly rebels against the established mores of patriarchal setup despite all her social criticism.

When the play begins, Nazia has been portrayed as a frail, wrinkled woman in her eighties. Though she is aware of her fall from grace yet she remains a go-getter. She abandons a film shooting when the director of the film, Sanjay wants to restrict her to a single line. When she came to know that Sanjay has not made any changes according to her, she reads out the mail to Vinay, the assistant that she had sent:

> Here is the mail I sent him. Dear Sanjay, about the family scene. I am the matriarch. I feel I need to deliver that punch.... Times have changed and you need to recap. (4)

These words uttered by Nazia reverberate the yearning of women to change and subvert the power structures that deny them space by transforming themselves into power generating and transmitting communities. Sanjay isn't willing to change the script for Nazia so she becomes angry and leaves the role. She acquires a defiant attitude towards him and succeeds in breaking the constraints binding her. She expresses:

> This is it. There is always a time in your life that the truth strikes you. (*a moment of realization for her*) Why didn't I see it? What am I doing here? I don't belong here. (taking off her wig) No more grandma roles for me. I'm going back to the theatre! Dancing! That's it. I am leaving. (4)

Commenting on the recognition of the self as the starting point for women's liberation, Greer avers, "She could begin not by changing the world, but by reassessing herself" (*The Feminine Mystique* 4). Nazia frees herself from the saree that she was wearing and wears a Kaftan which signifies that recognition of oneself should become the means of cognition. She articulates her feelings and expresses her longing for theatre:

> No matter what, nobody can take away the dances you've already had...I want more dances. Dances that nobody can take from me. Oh! this van is too small! It can't take my dancing. Your cinema is too small for me. My life is big. I am BIG and GENEROUS! Only the theatre deserves me! (5)

These words of Nazia highlight her indulgence in introspection and her attempt to develop a whole and harmonious self, at both intellectual and emotional levels. She realizes that this space is too narrow for her to negotiate and she needs to go back to the larger than life stage musicals of the 50s she used to be a part of in order to touch the essence of her art. She announces her intention to revive the play *Shakuntala* through a gutsier retelling. Nazia takes auditions for her new production—the revival of *Abhigyan Shakuntalam*, the poster with the title SHAKU! She had a theatre group in the past whose co-founder was her sister, Zarine who died during the communal riots. No matter what gruesome aspect of humanity she faced, she is determined to revive her theatre group with a new name i.e. 'Post-modern Indian theatre'.

Dattani has used the technique of flash back in the play to merge the interior and exterior personalities of the characters into a single whole. Nazia was playing the role of Shakuntala and her co-star Suhel was Dushyant during a theatrical performance in Pakistan when the horrors of partition were being felt. During the performance, suddenly pandemonium breaks out and a woman from the troupe shouted that they should not allow Hindus in the troupes who are to be migrated to India. Nazia's character changes from a meek Shakuntala to an assertive woman when she declares that there is no Hindu in the group "except artistes". Nevertheless, the insulting words of mob which represents the societal mindset do not waver her and she handles the situation with a firm hand by proving her strength.

> We know the kind of plays you put up, prancing around naked on the stage. And then, you move around with that Hindu. Whores like you will not find no place even in Hell! (16)

These words of the mob represent patriarchal ideology where women are blamed for every situation. Although Suhel resents and searches for some weapon, Nazia shows swiftness of action and shoots the miscreant and saves Suhel. She advises Suhel to go to Delhi and expresses her desire to join him but Suhel objects to that:

> Nazia. I'm going with you Suhel. Now.
>
> Suhel. No. It's too dangerous.
>
> Nazia. I don't care. I would rather die with you than live without you. (17)

Nazia convinces her sister to migrate with her to Delhi where they can fulfill their dreams of launching a theatre group against the wish of their father. She condemns the patriarchal code of conduct by liberating herself and does not marry according to the will of her father and also advises her sister to realise her own individuality:

> Don't be so foolish! Always dithering. For once in your life make a decision that will do some good. Obedient girls like you always end up in unhappy marriages.... Well you make up your mind now. (19)

The forced migration and widespread communal violence bear-testimony to the dehumanization of mankind during partition. Nazia had to pay a big price for her decision to migrate with Suhel. The killing of her sister because she gave her burqa to Nazia when the intruders attacked the train was a bone-chilling incident and raised numerous unanswered questions in Nazia's mind. Nazia recollects the gory incident and the innocence of her sister:

> She gave me her burqa! She was always the one who was uncertain. She was always afraid of making a wrong decision! But now—She did not think twice! There was no doubt in her mind.... (50)

Through the episode of Zarine's killing and Nazia's gang rape, Dattani portrays the gravity of sexual violence which women's bodies were subjected to during partition. Such treatment of women was the outcome of patriarchal power where women have always been treated as instruments for men to display their power and honour. Nazia expresses the brutality of men who treated her as an object to prove their victory over the other community:

> The butchers were on her and all the others. Suhel dragged me away. We walked all the way to the border. We crossed the border after bribing someone. But.... You see...I was still wearing that piece of black cloth. But we were in another country, with a different set of demons. They came at us. They came at me. They pushed me down behind the bushes. Five or six or seven, eight of them. I don't know. They tore at my clothes and at my flesh. All I could think of is why isn't Suhel saving me? These are his people! I stopped looking at those eyes, so much anger and hatred! Hell bent on humiliating me. I stared back with hatred too, but they hurt me even more till—I stopped looking into their eyes. (50)

These words reveal the fact that these violent acts treat women bodies as territory to be conquered, claimed or marked by the assailants. Being extremely vulnerable, women become easy targets of every form of oppression. Women's lives became the subject of patriarchal control during the riots when the partition of the country was actively under consideration. There was no longer a direct relationship between a human being and a nation state but it became, for women, a gendered relationship via religion and patriarchy, to the nation-state. The woman's body, as Veena Das points out:

> Became a sign through which men communicated with each other. The lives of women were framed by the notion that they were to bear permanent witness to the violence of partition. Thus, the political programme of creating the two nations of India and Pakistan was inscribed upon the bodies of women. (*Critical Events* 56)

Nazia musters courage to come out of the trauma and makes a new beginning where she refuses to accept patriarchal boundaries. She abandons Suhel who was the silent witness when her body was being treated as a territory to show male hegemony. The launch of her new play "Shaku" symbolizes her liberation from the appalling past. She offers the role of Dash—Dushyant to Vinay. The call of Suhel brings back the pain of her festering wound and she laments:

> You think it is so simple?... Things don't get finished. They just hide in as dark corner like a ghoul and grab at you when you are not looking. And sometimes you have to beat the shit out of the ghoul to make it crawl back into the dark corner. (24)

These words of Nazia highlight that independence makes little sense in the lives of women like her for whom the freedom of the country is tethered to betrayal by their families, by the nation, and more substantially, by the loss of control over their bodies and the erosion of consent. Commenting on the violence women were subjected to and the responses generated from the women-victims of Partition, a noted critic, Veena Das pertinently comments:

> The violence of the Partition was folded into everyday relations and that the events of Partition came to be incorporated into the temporal structure of relationships. (220)

Nazia has adjusted herself to the contingencies of life by indulging herself in the world of theatre but she expresses her fractured relationship and her resentment to Suhel in her words:

> We are not who we were. And I think it is a good thing. Of course I wish I were as beautiful as I was. And I wish you were too. We were both beautiful but—what's the point now? It's over. No point. Cobwebs. (25)

Nazia remembers the past when they both were together playing the role of Shakuntala and Dushyant but there was frustration and discontentment in their relation. Nazia convinced Suhel that she has left her home, her country for him but Suhel replies, "You left Lahore because you knew you will have a better chance of starting your company here..." (28). Nazia's rejection of her husband's false excuses and her quest for recognition is satiated through her words:

> Oh so I am helpless? And I need you to help me? So you can take control over my life. Oh there are too many women in dance and theatre who have succumbed to those tactics. Too many who allow men to ruin their lives.... I certainly don't need your help in bringing about my destruction! (29)

Therefore, Nazia develops an independent identity with her own aims in life, makes her own choices with a sense of responsibility. She is no longer fearful, dependent and suffering in silence. Commenting on the attempt of women who struggle for self-realization, Germaine Greer asserts:

> A woman has only to depart from the stereotype to find herself subjected to all kinds of discrimination and insult, although she may minimize it still for her own mental health. (*The Female Eunuch* 300)

Nazia leaves behind all the traces of her traumatic past, abandons her daughter born out of the mutilation of her body but is constantly haunted by the past. Her daughter, Ruby too is portrayed by Dattani as an unconventional woman who despite her rejection by her mother and husband becomes educated, self-reliant and brings up her daughter, Nikhat. However, her only quest is to establish identity of her dead mother as a result she undergoes mental agony and struggles to search her true identity:

> Everyone said my mother died after giving birth to me.... Even as a little girl, being handed over from an actress backstage to a seamstress to the washerwoman. They fed me all the time. But I was only a pair of hands that could sew, or mend or bring in cushions and flowers or hand over a bouquet to the chief guest.... I didn't exist. Everyone sympathized with me. Poor girl, her own aunt doesn't want to look at her. (46)

Nazia's revelation of Ruby's parentage is painful both for the mother and the daughter and reflects the agony of a rape victim. She suffers from some inconceivable upheaval within her and further expresses her trauma and her existence ranging between abject self-negation and aggressive self-assertion:

> You were my flesh, wounded, humiliated. I didn't cry when you came out. I was relieved—that the tapeworms infesting my belly left by those pigs who ate at my flesh, were out of my body. When Suhel gave you to me, he persisted and I resisted. He did not understand that if I held you—that I could just take my veil, wrap it around your neck and snap that tiny neck—get rid of you and my pain. Not because I hated you, but because I hated myself.... (52)

Nazia's resilience is reflected in her move to rehearse her new play with a radical improvisation and adaptation. Dattani has portrayed her as a woman who tries to create a world of her own choice with the will to explore herself by shaking the edifice of male supremacy. She rejects social ostracism and makes her character Shaku as an embodiment of woman's courage to fight, to question and to rebel. Nazia's Shaku rises in conflict unlike her mythical counterpart who succumbed to the patriarchal domination and meekly accepted the injustice as her fate. Nazia's interpretation of Shaku is her rebellious way of revisiting the male hegemony in the institution of marriage:

> You see, this is the interpretation I always wanted from Shakuntala! Not this whiny little creature whose entire future depends on whether husband can remember having slept with her or not. (37-38)

Nazia vehemently opposes sexual politics which operates in marriage and realizes that in a patriarchal society "to be born a female...is to be born into servitude" (Beauvoir 90). That is why, Nazia who once felt a great sense of achievement in performing the role of Shakuntala, brings about a complete reversal of the character.

In addition to the woman protagonist, the dramatist gives two more women characters who resemble the protagonist in their outlook and reflect the writer's viewpoint. Nikhat, Ruby's daughter is a young woman in her twenties and is a student of theatre at Yale. She proposes to play the role of Shakuntala to pay a tribute to her grandmother. Nikhat also feels the pain which her mother underwent and expresses the upheaval in her life to her mother:

> You gave what you got. Oh you were always around at home, trying to compensate and make sure I didn't go through the same feeling of abandonment. But even when you were holding my hand waiting for the school bus to pick me up, you too were thousands of miles away. Other mothers, talked to their daughters. Asked about their homework, their teachers, their friends but you never did. There was that whole week when you would give me my lunch box without packing my lunch in it, and at lunch break, I would open an empty lunch box. (47)

Dattani through the predicament of his women characters portrays that women are always conditioned by the patriarchal society to conform to the established norms of patriarchy but they have to understand that conformity is the bane of creativity and one has to fight against it. Both Nazia and Ruby have tried to search for an authentic, unitary self against the forces of fragmentation and alienation that threaten to undermine their veracity. All of them perform the play SHAKU, produced by Ruby. All these women join hands in projecting a powerful Shakuntala which is their collective effort to articulate women's point of view. Ruby applauds Nazia, the brain behind this creation when she says, "...there is no one as remarkable, bold, courageous and above all honest a person as my...." (54)

Nazia is a woman of substance and she could only achieve this due to her revolt against the authority of men be it abandoning her husband, her child and the veil which restricts the growth of women. The veil takes on different roles and connotations throughout the play and Dattani has used the veil as a distance between men and women, the veil of modesty, the veil which shrouds reality. Nazia has lived life to some extent on her own terms, who took on the stage as a profession because there was a stigma attached that it was nothing less than prostitution.

Ostensibly, Nazia shows that the identity of a female can be redefined by bringing to the fore its positive potential which can deconstruct the dominant concept of the male as absolute human subject and the subsidiary assumptions that validate it. She expresses her distinctiveness in her thank you note:

> I know many of you geriatrics out there remember me for my role as Shakuntala.... I don't think I was right for the part. It belonged to my sister. A very kind, beautiful, generous, evolved soul. Like Shakuntala. Something I can never be in this lifetime. But what the hell. Who wants to be generous and evolved when you have two dancing feet...Oops. Mine are unavailable, temporarily. But that won't keep me from dancing. (She begins to sway and clap) Dance away! And act like life is one big performance with a standing ovation waiting at the end of it! Spin me around! Oh this wheelchair is too small for all the life that's left in me. (55)

Women's are the dissonant voices which are ordinarily deflected, ignored, subordinated, excluded or destroyed. But Dattani through his women protagonist Ruby in *Where Did I Leave My Purdah?* registers protest against the unreasonable and irrational control of social conventions that do not permit women to articulate their feelings. His women characters make bold endeavor for recognition of their qualities and an appreciation of their contribution to society. They begin to rise in conflict against their tormented selves, against men and society. Dattani powerfully portrays the strong emotions of religious freedom and resentment by using the vision of his characters, particularly females. He uses his female characters to exhibit their internal enigmatic narratives of freedom at the same time depicting the religious hostility held by them. He attempts to articulate the voices of those women whose voices have remained inarticulate so far and they have evolved from woman who is circumscribed in the frames of the system to woman who battles with the dominant structures of power.

Works Cited

Bagchi, Jasodhara, and Subhoranjan Dasgupta. 'Introduction.' *The Trauma and the Triumph: Gender and Partition in Eastern India*. Ed. Bagchi and Dasgupta. Kolkata: Stree, 2009. 1-14. Print.

Beauvoir, Simone de. *The Second Sex*. Trans. Constance Borde and Sheila Malovan Chevallier. London: Vintage, 2010: 90. Print.

Das, Veena. *Critical Events; An Anthropological Perspective on Contemporary India*. New Delhi: OUP, 1995: 56. Print.

Dattani, Mahesh. *Where Did I Leave My Purdah?* 2012. Prime Time Theatre, Mumbai (Unpublished). (All further references have been cited from this source.)

Graeber, Laurel. "The Seeds of Partition." *New York Times*. 6 October 1991, BR 11.

Greer, Germaine. The Female Eunuch. London: Harper Perennial, 2006: 4. Print.

Menon, Ritu and Kamla Bhasin. *Borders & Boundaries*. New Delhi: Kali for Women and Women Unlimited, 1998: 41. Print.

19

Meaninglessness of Existence in *The Big Fat City*

Rashmi Sahi

Jean-Paul Sartre by proclaiming, "Man is nothing else but that which he makes of himself" (Sartre 29), nailed human beings with the impossible and improbable task of defining themselves, making them inescapable from the responsibility of their choices in the world. The life spent in frivolous gay abandonment, with all the caution to the wind, as if there was no tomorrow could be then labeled as irresponsible choices of man in a world where not only is he responsible for his own individuality, "but that he is responsible for all men" (Sartre 29) too.

This collectiveness of freedom (or imprisonment) and responsibility of a group complicates the already complex situation, more like ill-fitted jigsaw puzzle pieces displaying a deformed face. Yet, it also reinstates the partial albeit contorted authority of individuals on their destiny and its outcome through their 'control' on their free will. Sartre further goes on to say, "It is the act which decides its ends and its motives and the act is the expression of freedom" (Sartre 182), act being the choice made by an individual in a given situation. To flee from responsibilities is to tear away from the very essence of being. However, to take responsibility in a world where human beings suffer from 'abandonment' from an absent God, is no easy task. It is this feeling of abandonment which robs meaning from human suffering and renders life meaningless and purposeless.

Yet, to lead a life without purpose is to herald the very premises of existential angst leading to frustration, alienation and despair of many other things.

Although since the time of essence and existence, this profound meaninglessness has been at the core of most human problems, yet living in 21st century, in the age of information and technology this problem is extremely profound. As Kierkegaard describes, "Every age has its own particular immorality: 'the morality of our age is perhaps not lust, pleasure and sensuality, but rather a degenerate and pantheistic contempt for the individual'" (Solomon 361) and despair over being human.

This despair of existence and its accompanying problems are a major theme of the Sahitya Akademi Winner, Indian playwright, Mahesh Dattani's plays. His plays are a mirror of chaotic, debased human society full of meaningless wandering souls, governed by either stifling norms and limits of the society or encumbered with limitless freedom, as if human beings were, "condemned to be free" (Sartre 32), and as if they were "left alone without excuse" (Sartre 32).

In a world devoid of any proof of tangible God, Dattani's characters are left without any values and commands that would legitimate their behaviour. His plays sometimes are a soul piercing cry of existential angst of individuals, for they are replete with characters suffering from dread, boredom, alienation, freedom, commitment, nothingness and frustration, all the ailments springing from purposelessness and meaninglessness of life.

His latest play, *The Big Fat City* is no different. Set in the Indian metropolitan city of Mumbai, the play is a classic example of intense existential crisis in the lives of the characters, a desperate plea by couples, Nikarika-Murli, Lalita or Lolly-Mahesh, Anu-Puneet and Sailesh, the long lost friend of Murli. Their world is a world in which:

> Unlike an animal, man is not told by drives and instincts what he must do. And in contrast to man in former times, he is no longer told by traditions and values what he should do. Now, knowing neither what he must do nor what he should do, he sometimes does not even know

> what he basically wishes to do. Instead, he wishes to do what other people do—which is conformism—or he does what other people wish him to do—which is totalitarianism. (Frankl 194)

In *The Big Fat City*, both conformism and totalitarianism are at their full display. Niharika and Murli, the cash strapped couple, living in what Dattani describes in his stage setting, as "A compact 1 bedroom hall kitchenette. We see it all including the balcony of the bedroom and also the tiny loo" (1) giving it a sense of claustrophobic space rather than security of a home. Their house stands for their identity and status in the society; the small house diminishing their status on the social ladder as embarrassed Niharika says to Sailesh, "Everyone we know is moving into bigger better homes" (6). It is also the same house, where the entire saga of sad human drama takes place. The atmosphere in the house is loaded with the acrid smell of dread, of being left behind in the rat race of the modern life. If that is not enough, Murli loses the job that he has so proudly identified himself with. Joblessness in the society is equated to uselessness, further increasing the despair and frustration. How the inability of the newly unemployed Murli to pay mortgage of the flat, starts an unfortunate sequence of uncontrollable events, turning this desperate yet innocent situation into a saga of murder (Mahesh, Lolly's husband) and of honour killing (of Anu and Puneet), reeks of absurdity of life. The events actually bring forth the image of Camus' Sisyphus, "straining to push his rock up the mountain, watching it roll down, then descending after the rock to begin all over, in an endless cycle" (Aronson). The viciousness of the cycle and the desperation of gaining advantage over others plus finding no reason and meaning in this whole suffering, the characters are poster people of a meaningless life. "We are left alone, without excuses" (Sartre 32). This abandonment encumbered with meaninglessness spells doom in this play.

Sailesh, the newly reunited friend of Murli has his own desperation. Losing his job to his greed of making a quick buck, he comes to meet Murli with his own agenda. There he meets Lalita Jagtiani aka Lolly, yesteryears TV star, whose stars are fading. A believer of instant things, she forges an instant relationship with the star struck, Sailesh, getting "really cozy with Sailesh," (12) and planting, "a kiss on his cheeks" (12) as soon as they meet. Both being married to other people doesn't deter either from the open display of 'affection'. "Lolly first gets a little amorous and then uncontrollably so. She kisses him hard on the mouth" (38).

Lolly who is out of work, lacking funds and desperate to maintain the lifestyle of the rich and famous of her family, gets entangled with the underworld drug mafia. Her 'wayward' and confused teenage son, Rahul in the midst of a busted rave party organised by Lolly at their house, is first taken away by the police and then kidnapped by mafia. All this while, Lolly well knowing the state of her son, is busy in covering her own back and does nothing. The exchange of electronic messages between mother and son during the traumatic times somehow dehumanizes this beautiful relationship, creating a rift and symbolizing the changing dynamics of this all-loving and sacrificing relationship. His haunting message to Lolly, "Why mom? What did I do to deserve this?" (55) sends shiver down the spine.

Adding to more woes, on the fateful day, her husband, Kailesh Jagtiani, an alcoholic, who somehow ends in Niharika's and Murli's flat, is disposed in the bedroom of the flat which is actually occupied by Anu, an aspiring TV actress and her meek and spineless boyfriend, Puneet who are staying as paying guests under the guise of Niharika's relatives. Shallowness of the relationship, of Anu and Puneet, based on distrust leads to the murder of Kailesh by Puneet as Puneet accuses Anu, "Sleeping with strange men will not give you love! I will give you love!" (20). The conversation between Puneet and Anu after the murder is a perfect example of defilement of the emotion of love, debasement of individuals and debauchery of human beings.

> Niharika: He is dead.
>
> Anu (to Puneet): You—did this for me? You killed a man for me?
>
> Puneet: Yes, sweetheart.
>
> Anu: Oh, sweetheart!
>
> (Anu and Puneet embrace.) (20)

To even try and make sense of this, would need strength to be unbiased for the callousness of the reactions stop one in the tracks and forces one to think about the major collapse the humanity is heading towards. Thank God, "God doesn't exist" or if He does and if, "...each individual is the realization of a certain conception which dwells in the divine understanding," (Sartre 28), then the whole concept of the divinity is flawed. The meaning of such actions and reactions are beyond the realm of good or bad, it is the catastrophe that has befallen on men.

The casualness of Kailesh's murder is mouthed by Sailesh while comforting Lolly,

> Lolly, you have had a hard night I know. First the tragic news of your husband, then the raid where your son is being tested for drugs, and a missing packet that clearly you value above all the others. (37)

The struggle of individuals as individuals is evident from the value placed on the relationships and things. The choices made by the characters in *The Big Fat City*, as they have an external loci in transitory objects like money, status, short-term relationships further leads to the collective doom of the group. It is the choices made by individuals that ultimately affect the whole group. Sartre helps to understand the relationship between individual choices and group as,

> ...it puts every man in possession of himself as he is and places the entire responsibility for his existence squarely upon his own shoulders. And when we say that man is responsible for himself, we do not mean that he is responsible for his own individuality, but that he is responsible for all men. (Sartre 29)

The collective disgust of the group is also conspicuous through the cold blame game played over the murder of Kailash.

> Anu (to Sailesh): "You killed him because of your affair with Lolly." (42)
>
> Puneet (to Lolly): "I killed your husband. I found him sleeping with my girlfriend." (42)
>
> Unmatchable is Lolly's reaction to all this, "What are you mad??? Kailash hasn't slept with anything except the

> bottle in the last ten years." (suddenly patting Sailesh) "Oh darling. I am so happy I found you...." (Dattani 42)

It is not surprising that this brutality and blunting of emotions of the society and its alienation from the core human values are an extreme reflection of absurdism of abandonment in a godless world. According to Wikipedia the absurd is "the conflict between (a) the human tendency to seek inherent value and meaning in life and (b) the human inability to find" them.

Indeed no meaning or purpose is found either in life or in death. The murder then truly becomes a pawn amongst the guilt parched individuals, trying to milk some money from the situation. The hollowness of the human consciences and desensitized emotions are seen when Lolly ponders on Kailash's murder, "Oh Sailesh! When I saw Kailash's body on the floor—I knew he had left to make way for better things! I am so happy I don't need to feel guilty about anything!" (44). She later coolly haggles about money with Anu and her brother Harjeet, who has been called in from Anu's hometown Rewari on the pretext of producing a serial, in reality to compensate for the murder, money to reimburse for a lost human life.

Harjeet has come to Mumbai with his own agenda, to avenge the honour of his family and that of the Khap panchayat. His father has recently been elected the head of the panchayat and he has come as the messenger of yet another two deaths in the play, that of Anu and Puneet. The Khap panchayats, notorious for their honour killing of lovelorn couples, spare no one, not even when it comes to their own daughters as in this case of Anu. The mere idea of the human predicament hanging in the hands of a group of people, generates disgust and contempt and points towards fatalism, "the view that whatever a person's actions and circumstances, however free they may seem, his or her predetermined end is inevitable" (Solomon 438). The gory end of Anu and Puneet was predetermined by the Khap. One cannot derive any meaning out of these two young innocent deaths, nor from the escapist life they lead, loaning some time from their ultra-conservative families and trying to make a life on their own. The two confused souls, with their newly acquired lease of life are still leashed to their pegs, as Harjeet reacts to the situation,

> That's how the story needs to be. Sacrifice. The honour of the village is more important (59) finally pulling the trigger.

The play ends on a whimsical note from Niharika who while talking to Murli, sums up this meaningless saga, "You know we tried our best to keep this. We lied, we abetted a murder…you know, I could do that again if I can have this flat. It's a home. I can understand even killing for a home. But honour? Why would anyone kill for honour? I mean. What is it?" (61).

Lolly on the other hand, sells her own house, and settles into another meaningless relationship with Sailesh after buying a house for Sailesh's wife and her lover. The painting of Mumbai city, given by Lolly to Niharika as a parting gift symbolises the existential crisis in people's life in general, in which, "so many people just going about as if life was all about…getting somewhere" (61) reminds one of Sartre's views on freedom, "we are free, we are freedom, we are condemned to be free" (Sartre 176).

Works Cited

"Absurdism." *Wikipedia: The Free Encyclopedia.* Wikimedia Foundation, n.d. Web. 31 Jan. 2014.

Aronson, Ronald. "Albert Camus", *The Stanford Encyclopedia of Philosophy* (Spring 2012 Edition), Edward N. Zalta (ed.), *URL.* <http://plato.stanford.edu/archives/spr2012/entries/camus/>. Web. 31 Jan. 2014.

Dattani, Mahesh. *The Big Fat City.* Manuscript, Final Draft, 2013. (Unpublished). (The figures in brackets pertaining to the play are from this source.)

Frankl, Viktore E. *Man's Search for Meaning*. London: The Random House Group Ltd., 2008. Print.

Priest, Stephen (ed.). *Jean-Paul Sartre: Basic Writings*. New York: Routledge, 2001. Print.

Solomon, Robert C. *Introducing Philosophy*. Eighth. New York: Oxford University Press, 2005. Print.

20

The Big Fat City: 'Life in a Metro'

Lalit Ratoniya

A playwright, director, actor, dancer and teacher, Mahesh Dattani is one of those multi-talented personalities who have carved a niche for themselves in the world. His plays have infused freshness and enthusiasm in Indian theatre in English which was lagging behind the other literary genres for so long. He is the first playwright in English who was honoured with the Sahitya Akademi award in 1998. Dattani is an artist who wants to articulate the human emotions through his art. In the Preface to his book he himself writes, "I know I am an artist... I write for my plays to be performed and appreciated by as wide a section of the society that my plays speak to and are about" (*Collected Plays*, xi). With the help of his dramatic genius and theatrical ability, he has presented hidden and burning issues of the society on the stage. The characters, themes portrayed in his plays have universal appeal. He blends conventional themes with the modern approaches in his plays. Amarnath Prasad writes, "To me Mahesh Dattani comes in this category of writers who champion the cause of true art—free from any theory, universal in taste and flavour, appealing to all sections of society, never bound to any caste, class and creed" (69).

Dattani has addressed a number of social concerns in his plays such as gender discrimination, gender identity, communal tensions, child sexual abuse, ill treatment of marginalized sections like eunuchs and homosexuals etc. But, what makes his plays distinctive is the fact that all his plays are the portrayal of the urban milieu of India. He explores the problems and issues of the urban locale. He explains the reason for depicting the urban milieu in his plays in the following way,

> I think the old cliché about writing what you know best holds good for any work or for any art (drama or literature). I think one has to be true to one's own environment. Even if I attempted writing a play about the angst of rural Indian society, it wouldn't ring true, it would be an outsider's view—I could only hope to evoke sympathy, but never to really be a part of that unless I spend a lot of time there. I think there are enough issues and challenges in urban Indian society (the milieu I am a part of) and these automatically form the content of my work. (qtd. in Mee 156-57)

As Dattani himself was born and brought up in urban India the stories of his plays come directly from that part of country. His characters are rooted in the urban multi-ethnic setting of modern middle class of India. The places which he has chosen for the setting are mostly the metro-cities of India. *The Big Fat City* (2013), his latest play, too tries to capture the essence of life in one of the most fascinating metropolitan cities of India, i.e. Mumbai.

The present paper aims to critically analyse the play *The Big Fat City*. It also proposes to examine the challenges and issues faced by the urban middle class people for their existence in the metropolitan cities as portrayed by Dattani in the play.

Mumbai, the sprawling metropolis, the economic capital of India is synonymous with ambition and a drive for professional success and money-making. It is a melting pot of cultures where people come from all over the country with their hopes and dreams. But, ultimately they are caught up in a fiercely competitive struggle for wealth and power which leads to the loss of human values. Taking inspiration from the present day scenario of Mumbai and many such metro-cities, Mahesh Dattani has written and directed his latest play, *The Big Fat City*. In an interview given to Deepa Punjani he says about Mumbai being his inspiration for the play,

> I lived in Lokhandwala for a good three years. It was in a milieu of aspiring actors, musicians, filmmakers, corporate executives recently transferred to Mumbai. A very motivated lot of young people waiting for the right move or contact to take them a step closer to stardom, fortune or that penthouse in Oberoi towers. Success has to be worn on one's sleeve, so one always aspired to graduate to Bandra. What they say about New York City can be tweaked to fit Mumbai. I can say, in Lokhandwala, everyone is looking for an apartment, a role and a lover. And when they have these then they are looking for a better apartment, a better role and a better lover. It is in this mobile, culturally and morally flexible class of people that I found inspiration. After all, there is certain honesty even in their pretensions. Their objectives are clearly defined and so are their obstacles. (qtd. in Punjani 2013)

Thus, the play revolves around the urban middle class people living in Mumbai and their lives and lifestyles. The theme of the play is very close to the theme of a critically acclaimed film, Life in a Metro directed by Anurag Basu which narrates the individual lives of nine people living in Mumbai. But, the treatment of both these two medium is different as the film is a pure drama whereas Dattani's play is a black comedy. He himself writes, "*The Big Fat City* is a play that may have all the elements of a knockabout farce but is in fact a black comedy on the sad, lonely but stimulating lives that we lead in the city of dreams" (*Me and My Plays* 42).

The play is an amalgamation of three stories that come together with one dramatic incident. The story revolves around a corporate couple, Murli and Niharika, trying to pay off loan for their new apartment in a fancy suburb of Mumbai; an out-of-work television star, Lalita with a troublesome marriage and an aspiring young actress, Anu who has come from a small town and is staying with the couple. All the characters of the play are struggling hard to 'make it big' in this city. The play is set in the flat of Murli and his wife Niharika where they invite Sailesh, a banker and Murli's college friend, for dinner. As Murli has been fired from his job recently, he is unable to pay the monthly instalments of his loan on time. Niharika feels that Sailesh can help them out in this financial crisis and this is why she also calls her neighbour, a fading television actress Lalita or Lolly, to impress him. But, Sailesh has also come with the intention of asking money from Murli to settle a client's account. Lolly too is having problems in her life as she is not getting work anymore and is trying hard to meet her family's luxurious and extravagant lifestyle. This has also lead her to arrange a 'rave party' along with her son in her flat on that night where they have planned to sell drugs. The story takes a turn when Lolly's drunkard husband is mistakenly killed by Puneet, the possessive lover of Anu. To save Puneet, Anu offers huge sum of money to each one of them who has been a witness to the murder which can easily solve their monetary problems. So, in a bid to gain money, they all forget humanity and land up becoming accomplices in the murder. But the climax in the play comes at that moment when Harjeet, Anu's brother, comes to Mumbai from Haryana and to avenge family's honour kills both Anu and Puneet.

The Big Fat City is a sarcastic take on the new middle class society which is ready to go to any extent to fulfill their aspirations. The conscience of the characters portrayed in the play seems to be dead. They all are trying to use one another for their own benefits. Niharika pretends to feel happy to receive Sailesh in her house, but actually she is thinking of the help which Murli can ask from him. Sailesh too, calls Niharika, "A pretentious, snooty bitch" (160) in the text message sent to his wife. Relationships are of no value to these greedy people. When Niharika comments about Lolly, "Lolly is a dear, dear friend of mine and I would never agree to a remark like that!" (199), Anu does not wait for a second to say, "Oh, come on! It's all nonsense. As if you care about Lolly...I have lived in this city long enough to see beyond that crap, so don't give me that 'I care about Lolly' nonsense" (199). Even the relationship between husband and wife is not based on love and mutual trust. The audience is surprised to see Lolly's indifference towards her husband's death who quickly accepts Sailesh as the father of her son. Sailesh also openly professes his wife's affair with his neighbour,

> Lolly: Oh, Sailesh! When I saw Kailash's body on the street—I knew he had left to make way for better things! I am so happy I don't need to feel guilty about anything!
>
> Sailesh: Neither do I! My wife can now openly carry on with our neighbour. She will be so happy when I tell her! (218)

The grim reality of the modern age is revealed at that moment when the dead body of Kailash is tossed out of the balcony of the flat by Anu and Puneet without hesitation. Among all the witnesses, nobody even dissuades Anu from doing that which exposes the insensitivity and ruthlessness of the urban society. Also no one, including Kailash's wife Lolly, feels any remorse for the loss of a human life. In spite of that, they are more concerned with their personal problems. Therefore, the men and women portrayed in the play are actually pretentious, hypocrites, selfish and inhumane and eventually the play unveils what is behind their facades.

But all these characters have to pay the price for leading lives beyond their means. At the end Murli and Niharika have to leave the glitz and glamour of Mumbai and go to Thirunavelli. Anu does not survive to fulfill her dreams of becoming actress and marrying Puneet. Lolly has to sell her flat to pay drug mafia and her only son leaves her. These characters are the representatives of the urban middle class society which does not even care to forego their human values in their pursuit of money and success.

Dattani has dealt with the diverse contemporary issues in the play. The downfall of moral and ethical values, commodification of human relationships, struggle for existence, disintegration of marital relationships and adultery are some of the pertinent concerns of this fast paced world. Another major socio-cultural issue that has been discussed in the play is 'honour killing'. It may seem bizarre in the urban social set-up to kill a girl and her boyfriend for honour; as Niharika too says, "You know, we tried our best to keep this. We lied, we abetted a murder.... You know, I could do that again if I can have this flat. It's home. I can understand even killing for a home. But honour? Why would anyone kill for honour? I mean...what is it?" (244). But by depicting this, Dattani has brought out a sharp contrast between the priorities of small towns and metro cities. Both Harjeet and Niharika can kill anyone, one for the family honour and the other for a flat in suburb.

In *The Big Fat City*, Dattani has employed black comedy for the first time to explore social problems. He has skilfully juxtaposed humour with pathos to help his audience in coping up with the gloomy outlook of the modern world. The play has all the basic elements of black comedy whether it is humour, dramatic irony, satire, grotesque characters or the absurd actions leading to confusion. These elements not only evoke laughter but also give audience the food for thought. For example, in order to impress Sailesh, Niharika forces Murli to wear silk kurti in which he feels uncomfortable,

> Murli: Can't I wear my regular shirt, please?
>
> Niharika: Stop fidgeting with that kurti. You will tear it. No, you can't.... It's torn! (Most upset) One chance! We have this one chance and you want to ruin it? (156-58)

The conversation between them compels audience to laugh and at the same time shows the artificiality of the urban society. Dattani says, "The events are rather tragic but the mode is completely comic. At times you don't know whether to laugh or to recoil in horror or to offer sympathy or to just ridicule what's going on. There is rasa, there is a hasya, there is a karuna, there is raudra, there is everything. It is all in a platter—a kind of combination and you take it all in one" (qtd. in Sen 2012).

Dattani's plays are exceptionally thought-provoking as they reveal the complexities of modern day life. For this, he makes use of the new techniques in theatre that suits the theme and brings out the best in the play. In this play too, he has done innovation in the dramatic technique with the use of text messages. The text messages which are flashed on the screen help audience to understand the inner feelings of the characters and their thought process. For instance, Lolly's hypocrisy is revealed when she pretends in front of others that she is not interested in television anymore whereas she is actually begging for a role from one of the television producers to improve her declining career.

SCREEN (from Lolly): SORRY EKTA. BUT PLEASE, PLEASE GIVE ME A RUNNING CHARACTER IN YOUR NEW SERIAL. I REALLY DON'T WANT TO DO THAT MORBID DATTANI PLAY. I AM DESPERATE. PLEASE. (168)

Therefore, technology is used by the playwright to expose lies and pretensions of the characters which they try to maintain for their survival.

Thus, the play *The Big Fat City* scrutinizes the social and cultural realities of the urban milieu of India. Dattani delves deep into the lives and psyche of urban middle class people who are as hollow, artificial and materialistic as the world where they exist. He has also revealed the anxiety, confusion, desperation and frustration of the modern man who wants to achieve more in a short span of time at the cost of human values.

Works Cited

Dattani, Mahesh. Preface *Collected Plays*. New Delhi: Penguin Books, 2000, (xi-xv). Print.

———. "The Big Fat City". *Me and My Plays*. New Delhi: Penguin Books, 2014. Print. (All textual citations are taken from this edition.)

———. *Me and My Plays*. New Delhi: Penguin Books, 2014. Print.

Mee, Erin B. "Mahesh Dattani: Invisible Issues". *Mahesh Dattani's Plays: Critical Perspectives*. Ed. Angelie Multani. New Delhi: Pencraft International, 2007. Print.

Prasad, Amarnath. "The Plays of Mahesh Dattani: A Fine Fusion of Feeling and Form". *The Dramatic World of Mahesh Dattani: A Critical Exploration*. Ed. Amarnath Prasad. New Delhi: Sarup Book Publishers Pvt. Ltd., 2009. Print.

Punjani, Deepa. "Mahesh Dattani". *The Mumbai Theatre Guide.com*, 2013. Web. <http://www.mumbaitheatreguide.com/dramas/interviews/17-mahesh-dattani-interview.asp>

Sen, Debrati S. "Mumbai, Up, Close and Personal in Mahesh Dattani's Latest Play." *The Times of India*. December, 2012. Web. <http://timesofindia.indiatimes.com/entertainment/hindi/bollywood/news/Mumbai-up-close and-personal-in-Mahesh-Dattanis-latest-play/articleshow/17615833.cms>